ƒormatio

TRADITION. EXPERIENCE.
TRANSFORMATION.

Formatio books from InterVarsity Press follow the rich tradition of the church in the journey of spiritual formation. These books are not merely about being informed, but about being transformed by Christ and conformed to his image. Formatio stands in InterVarsity Press's evangelical publishing tradition by integrating God's Word with spiritual practice and by prompting readers to move from inward change to outward witness. InterVarsity Press uses the chambered nautilus for Formatio, a symbol of spiritual formation because of its continual spiral journey outward as it moves from its center. We believe that each of us is made with a deep desire to be in God's presence. Formatio books help us to fulfill our deepest desires and to become our true selves in light of God's grace.

THE RHYTHMS OF THE JESUS LIFE

Foreword by
EUGENE H. PETERSON

RAW
SPIRITUALITY

TOM SMITH

Afterword by
JAMES BRYAN SMITH

IVP Books

An imprint of InterVarsity Press
Downers Grove, Illinois

InterVarsity Press
P.O. Box 1400, Downers Grove, IL 60515-1426
World Wide Web: www.ivpress.com
Email: email@ivpress.com

InterVarsity Press® is the book-publishing division of InterVarsity Christian Fellowship/USA®, a movement of students and faculty active on campus at hundreds of universities, colleges and schools of nursing in the United States of America, and a member movement of the International Fellowship of Evangelical Students. For information about local and regional activities, write Public Relations Dept., InterVarsity Christian Fellowship/USA, 6400 Schroeder Rd., P.O. Box 7895, Madison, WI 53707-7895, or visit the IVCF website at www.intervarsity.org.

Scripture quotations, unless otherwise noted, are from The Message. Copyright © 1993, 1994, 1995. Used by permission of NavPress Publishing Group. All rights reserved.

While all stories in this book are true, some names and identifying information in this book have been changed to protect the privacy of the individuals involved.

Cover design: Cindy Kiple
Interior design: Beth Hagenberg
Images: old paper sheet: © robynmac/iStockphoto
         stack of pots: © rearwindowart/iStockphoto

ISBN 978-0-8308-3588-1 (print)
ISBN 978-0-8308-9652-3 (digital)

Printed in the United States of America ∞

Library of Congress Cataloging-in-Publication Data

Smith, Tom, 1975- May 28-
   Raw spirituality : the rhythms of the Jesus life / Tom Smith.
      pages cm
   Includes bibliographical references.
   ISBN 978-0-8308-3588-1 (pbk. : alk. paper)
   1. Christian life. 2. Jesus Christ. I. Title.
   BV4501.3.S6568 2014
   248.4—dc23
                    2014013399

P	25	24	23	22	21	20	19	18	17	16	15	14	13	12	11	10	9	8	7	6	5	4	3	2	1
Y	35	34	33	32	31	30	29	28	27	26	25	24	23	22	21	20	19	18	17	16	15	14			

In loving memory of Sulette Smith
(26.7.1949–12.4.2014),
who taught me to live in
the unforced rhythms of grace.

Contents

List of Figures

Foreword

—✒—

Tom Smith is relentless. He insists, no holds barred, that the Christian life necessarily *must be lived* using all our body parts, visible and invisible. There is not a hint of romanticism, idealism or perfectionism in what he writes. He just wants us to take seriously what has been handed down to us for two thousand years in Christian worship and witness and obedience.

In 2003 a few friends gathered together to form a worshiping congregation of Christians in Johannesburg, South Africa, the country where he had grown up. They named the church *Claypot*, taking the name from Paul's letter to the Corinthian church, "We carry this precious Message around in the unadorned clay pots of our ordinary lives" (2 Corinthians 4:7).

They found their focus early: Jesus. The focus of their worship and witness and obedience was to be Jesus, God in human form: flesh and bone, blood and muscle, lungs and stomach, heart and liver—the works. Not God as a good idea, not God as a promising program, not God as a set of rules to keep us on the straight and narrow, not God as inspiration to put zest in our lives.

Christians have never found it easy to maintain this Jesus focus, but the gospel writers insist on it. Jesus is human, like me, like you, like us. "No one has ever seen God; the only God [Jesus] ... has made him known" (John 1:18 ESV). God in human form, Jesus. A human form that I can verify simply by touching my nose, my elbow. A historical person on two legs who walked the paths and roads on the ground in Palestine in the first century just as I walk on sidewalks and trails in North America and South Africa. Jesus spent nine months in the womb just as I did. He was born of a woman just as I was. We know not only his name but the name of his mother. There was a family. There are named friends. There was work to do, carpentry and masonry and fishing. Meals were eaten. Dishes were washed. Prayers were prayed. He walked in and out of houses and synagogues and the temple just as we do in houses and schools and Walmarts and churches. He died and was buried, just as we will.

This takes a great deal of the guesswork out of knowing God. Do you want to know what God is like, the form in which God reveals himself? Look in the mirror, look at your friend, look at your spouse. Start here: a human being with eyes and ears, hands and feet, an appetite and curiosity, eating meals with your friends, walking to the store for a bottle of milk, hiking in the hills picking wildflowers, catching fish and cooking them on a beach for a breakfast with your children.

Four writers were assigned by God's Holy Spirit the task of writing down the story of this God-with-us, Jesus, who lived in first-century Palestine. They all write the same story with variations. But the one thing that they totally agree on is that this Jesus, this revelation of God, was an actual human person who lived his life in the identical conditions in which we live ours. No special effects, no dazzling angelic interventions, no levitations. Simple and thoroughly feet-on-the-ground ordinary. There was a brief moment, one night in a boat caught in a storm on Lake Galilee, it lasted maybe ten seconds at the most, when his friends thought he was a ghost, but they quickly realized they were wrong. There was a later occasion, three days after they had watched him die on a cross, when they thought that Jesus was a ghost. Wrong again. There was no question. Jesus was totally human, just like them.

In another New Testament piece of writing, the letter to the Hebrews, this thoroughly human Jesus is affirmed, but with one exception: he was "without sin" (Hebrews 4:15). Otherwise, he lived and experienced it all, everything that goes into the human condition: weakness, limitations, temptations, suffering, celebration, birth and death. What this means, and it is the task of the Christian community and its pastors to insist on it—and the people at Claypot and Pastor Tom Smith do insist on it—is that Jesus is not a principle or an idea or a truth, nothing abstract, nothing in general, nothing grandiose. When God revealed himself to us he did it in a human body.

There is, of course, more to it than this. Jesus is not *just* human; he is also divine. Not only very human but very God. But what we have to face first of all, and what the Gospel writers do face, is that the divinity does not overpower, doesn't diminish so much as by a fingernail, doesn't dilute even by as much as a teardrop, the humanity. This is a holy mystery, that Jesus at the same time that he is fully human with and for us is also God fully present to us, breathing the very Holy Spirit of God into us, enacting salvation and eternal life in us. But first of all—our four Gospel writers are emphatic about this—we are told in no uncertain terms that God became flesh in a named person, the human flesh of Jesus, and lived among us. We start with the human. This is the way God makes himself known to us.

⌁

You would think that this would be enthusiastically embraced as good news—unqualified good news. But when it comes right down to it I would rather be like God than that God be like me. It turns out that a lot of us, more times than we like to admit, aren't all that excited that a very human Jesus is revealing God to us. We have our own ideas of what we want God to be like. We keep looking around for a style of spirituality that gives some promise that we can be godlike, be in control of our lives and the lives of others, exercise godlike authority or at least be authorities on God.

When know-it-all Serpent promised our first parents that they could be "like God," you can be sure they were not thinking of anything human with all the limitations of being human. They were thinking of something far grander—knowing everything there is to know and getting an edge on the rest of the creation. When they heard those words from Serpent, "like God," we can easily imagine what went on in their heads: power, control, being in charge of everything, getting their own way, indulging every whim, able to do anything they desired without restriction.

The usual way in which we try to become like God is first to eliminate the God who reveals himself in human form and reimagine God as the god I want to be, invest this reimagined god with my own god fantasies, and then take charge of the god business.

The old term for this reimagined replacement god is idolatry. It is without question the most popular religion in town—any town—and it always has been. In previous generations these idolatry gods were made of wood and stone, of gold and silver. More often these days they are made of words and ideas, abstractions and principles, programs and projects. But the common element that defines them as idols is that they are nonhuman, nonpersonal, nonrelational. It is almost as if someone edited what St. John wrote from "The Word became flesh" to "The Word became a training manual, a project outline, a motivational paperback."

But idolatry always backfires—in an attempt to become godlike by becoming more than human, we become less human, nonhuman: those who make them are like them; so are all who trust in them (Psalm 115:8). You'd think we would learn.

There is a backstory here that is helpful in understanding Tom Smith's fierce focus and energetic imagination. He grew up in South Africa during the years of apartheid when the entire nonwhite population was excluded from a dominant Christian church, resulting in widespread oppression and poverty. He also was aware that the Rwanda genocide took place in a population mostly Christian. He became a pastor in a flourishing South African church and then came to North America. He experienced the temptation to degenerate church into a consumer program to attract customers. In both cultures names had been obscured by numbers and personal stories had been eroded by impersonal programs.

He returned to Johannesburg determined to avoid developing a congregation that is primarily about show and function. He gathered a few friends and developed a congregation around the metaphor *Claypot* and embarked on nurturing an imagination that takes the body of Christ, the *humanity* of Christ, what he names *raw* spirituality. This book is a witness to what takes place when names trump numbers, and stories with their accompanying metaphors keep relationships personal and prayerful.

About halfway through the reading of this manuscript I realized that it is a rewriting of St. Paul's message to the Christian congregation in Colossae where Paul insists that the life of Christ is intended to be lived in our lives in every detail; in his words, Christ *in you*, that's right, *in your* bodies as well as Christ's body (Colossians 1:27).

Eugene H. Peterson

Introduction

One day, while I sat in a coffee shop and worked on a weekend sermon, the waiter saw what I was working on and looked at me excitedly,

"Pastor, I have a problem," he said. "I accepted Jesus into my heart a few months ago and it is wonderful. I go to church every Sunday morning. But in the evenings I have wild promiscuous sex." He looked at me to gauge my reaction. Then he asked something that I will never forget. "I have accepted Jesus into my heart, but how do I get him into my penis?"

I have had many of these impromptu pastoral conversations, but I must confess that this was a first for me. Although his question was unconventional it showed the deep desire of a man who wants to be formed into Christlikeness in every part of his body.

You might find his statement shocking or even offensive, but I am convinced that if we are going to be transformed into the likeness of Jesus we will have to talk about every detail of our lives.

The apostle Paul wrote to the church in Rome, "Do not let any part of your body become an instrument of evil to serve sin. Instead, give yourselves completely to God, for you were dead, but now you have new life. So use your whole body as an instrument to do what is right for the glory of God" (Romans 6:13 NLT).

In this book we will explore a raw spirituality through which we become instruments doing "what is right for the glory of God." As we learn to use our bodies to the glory of God, this embodied faith extends into the world—making it a better place. This is raw spirituality.

HOW DISEMBODIED FAITH WRECKS OUR WORLD

I grew up in a church culture where it was all about "having Jesus in your heart." Churches were interested in getting Jesus into hearts and populating heaven with people who have Jesus in their hearts. There wasn't a lot of emphasis on the Jesus life through the rest of my anatomy and into everyday life. The Jesus life was disembodied.

It was this version of the Jesus story that allowed a gross system like apartheid to form in my home country, South Africa. We accepted Jesus into our hearts and worshiped him on Sunday, but during the rest of the week we used our bodies and the rest of our complex lives in ways that oppressed other people. We segregated Jesus from the raw material of our everyday life.

Many people have been hurt by versions of a disembodied Jesus story. Some have been oppressed by it, like the millions of people in South Africa. In other places this distortion led to genocide. In Rwanda, where a majority of the people "accepted Jesus into their hearts," people used their bodies to kill one another.[1]

Some of the hurts are not as obvious as the South African or Rwanda stories, but they are also deadly. I know a lot of people who have become bored with a disembodied version of Christianity; they have already accepted Jesus into their hearts, but what now? While I lived in the United States for three years I saw how this disembodied version got mixed with a consumerism wherein the temptation became to use Jesus like a product. Every Sunday people came to the church like they were shopping at a mall. The rawness of Christ's humanity morphed into a plastic consumer product.

I regularly meet people who feel sad about current versions of Christianity. Some of them say the Christian life is just a lot of chat, that the church suffers from verbal diarrhea, that it is all a head trip. Some of their sadness siphons into bitter anger or cynicism. They seek embodiment in other places.

Several of my friends feel the growing frustration of the gap between what they profess to believe and the actual rhythms of their everyday lives. The waiter in the restaurant falls in this group. He sincerely wants Jesus to become real in all of his life, but he experiences the disappointment of not knowing how. I share some of the hurt, sadness, boredom, frustrations and disappointments. I also yearn for something else.

In *Desiring the Kingdom* James K. A. Smith writes that

> one of the most crucial things to appreciate about Christian formation is that it happens over time. It is not fostered by events or experiences; real formation cannot be effected by actions that are merely episodic. There must be a rhythm and a regularity to formative practices in order for them to sink in.[2]

The raw spirituality described in this book is for those of us who want to learn how to embody the Jesus life through an engagement with rhythms within our everyday existence. In what follows I will describe how a group of us discovered these rhythms and sunk into raw spirituality.

DEVELOPING A RULE OF LIFE

In 2003, a few friends and I planted a church in Johannesburg, South Africa. Our church's name is Claypot; the name comes from a passage Paul wrote to the Corinthian church. "We carry this precious Message around in the unadorned clay pots of our ordinary lives" (2 Corinthians 4:7).

As a community we were drawn to this verse because we were frustrated with continual church critique. We wondered what it would look like to spend our time focusing on Jesus instead of obsessing over the vessel. Raw spirituality starts with God.

One day Jesus was approached with the eternal question "What is the good life?" He answered,

> The first is, "Hear, O Israel: the Lord our God, the Lord is one; you shall love the Lord your God with all your heart, and with all your soul, and with all your mind, and with all your strength." The second is this, "You shall love your neighbor as yourself." There is no other commandment greater than these. (Mark 12:29-31 NRSV)

Jesus wants to be in our hearts. He also desires to be in the rest of our lives in such a way that we become an embodying presence of his love. In order to train us in embodying loving God with heart, soul, mind and strength we developed a rule of life. For us a rule of life consists of Jesus' invitations that we follow together. The rule of life provides a general rhythm; its implications are as unique as the individuals partaking in it and the contexts they find themselves in.

Marjorie Thompson describes a rule of life as "a pattern of spiritual disciplines that provides structure and direction for growth in holiness."[3] A rule of life is a way to orient and train our lives toward God. Through our rule of life we seek to embody a raw spirituality for the sake of the world.

But what does this mean practically?

For us it means a life engaged with seven invitations, or what we call the rhythms. Our love for God, neighbors and ourselves flows out into engagement with the rhythms to (1) develop healthy images of God as number one in our lives, (2) plugging in daily, (3) journeying with other people, (4) discovering our piece of the puzzle and gifting others with it, (5) placing ourselves in other people's shoes, (6) commitment to downward mobility and servitude, and (7) seeing our working lives as an essential expression of our with-God life. An honest engagement with every rhythm fosters raw spirituality. It is a way of embodying the life of Jesus.

The rhythm of life diagram represents the raw spirituality we are going to explore (see fig. 1.1).

Figure 1.1. Rhythm of Life

Our exploration will start with some general training tips. Then we will move into the rhythm starting at the center. God initiates the rhythm. We will then circle around to the other rhythms. We will conclude our journey with an example of how you can contextualize a raw spirituality within your local community.

HOW TO USE THIS BOOK

As I wrote this book my wife repeatedly said, "Tell them that we cannot do this alone." She is right. Developing raw spirituality is not a solo affair. This book describes a journey within the environment of encouraging friendships. Raw spirituality also involves training. Following Jesus exposes us to the verbs of *practice, exercise, training* and *discipline*. In this book I will use the umbrella term *training naked* for these vibrant verbs. In the first chapter I will explain the concepts of training naked further.

In every chapter you will find input followed by a "Training Naked" section, which includes questions and training exercises. If you are like me, you might be tempted to read this book but skip the training exercises and the questions. I encourage you not to do that. All three aspects are crucial.

Invite a few friends to go on this journey with you (at least one but not more than seven). Decide on a day, time and place where you can hang out. Without companionship, questing with the questions and training with the exercises of this book will become just another head trip. Adri-Marie, my friend and colleague, is fond of saying that too much information in the head without an embodying in life makes the heart sick. I suggest that you first read chapters one, two and three, and after that you can skip around in the book.

One more thing: Read this book in unusual spaces. Raw spirituality develops in unusual physical locations. Find a raw space like a park, school, wilderness area or off-the-map coffee shop. Relocate your body. Move away from comfort.

May this book help you to develop an embodied raw spirituality that makes the world a better place. Glory to the Father and to the Son and to the Holy Spirit, as it was in the beginning, is now and will be forever. Amen.

ONE

Training Naked

*Stay clear of silly stories that get
dressed up as religion. Exercise daily in God—
no spiritual flabbiness, please!*

1 Timothy 4:7

*You cannot be a pew potato
and simultaneously engage in spiritual
formation in Christ's likeness.*

Dallas Willard

In our first year of marriage Lollie and I lived close to a convenience store. It was a short five-minute walk. We always drove. As a newly married couple we cultivated the habit of going to the store after dinner and buying some treats. The law of consumption states that calories accumulate.

One evening while we were brushing our teeth I noticed that I had lengthened in width. My love handles were offering extra grips to Lollie. I expanded sideways. Unfortunately this wasn't the only thing I noticed. I saw small bubbles that formed underneath my skin. In horror I called Lollie and asked her what she thought it was, maybe chickenpox? Lollie carefully inspected the bubbles on my skin and then exclaimed, "It is cellulite!" I thought she was wrong; cellulite was a woman's issue, right? I was wrong—I had cellulite.

I had become flabby. Acknowledging my flabbiness was the first step toward a healthier life. The reality was that I was a twenty-something male with cellulite and huge love handles. How would I handle it? We ended our trips to the convenience store and made an appointment with a dietitian. I also contacted someone who could help me with an exercise program so I could train my body and lose the cellulite and love handles.

When Paul writes to Timothy he tells him to watch out for irreverent, silly myths. Eugene Peterson paraphrases it as "spiritual flabbiness." Before Timothy's community could exercise toward godliness they had to face the spiritual flabbiness circulating in their culture. They had to combat spiritual cellulite.

The Greek word Paul uses for exercise or train is *gymnazō*. It is where we get our word *gymnasium*. The verb Paul uses literally means to "exercise naked."[1] Greek gymnasiums were an atrocity to the Jews because men and women exercised there in the nude, and the rabbis warned against the "immorality of the baths."[2]

Why would Paul use such a provocative image that combines training and nakedness?

Paul used this gymnasium image because growth starts from a place of raw honesty and openness. From this honesty we are able to move into training. As we honestly face the cellulite in our lives, we engage in training. The journey begins with a glance in the mirror or standing on a scale. From here we move into training.

What would it look like if our churches became movements in which we exercise naked? When I just typed that last sentence I first wrote, "What would it look like if our churches became *places* where we exercise naked?" I retyped that because I think part of the problem that feeds into a disembodied version of the Jesus story is an imagination deficit. When we think of church, we tend to think of a building and a specific time of the week. Our imaginations link the word *church* with a building visited on a Sunday.

If we are going to move toward an embodying of Jesus in our everyday life, we have to imagine church as more than just this place and time. Discovering the church as a grace-filled gymnasium is a good starting place.

CHURCH AS A GRACE-FILLED GYMNASIUM

As a father of two children under the age of eight, I have been conferred with a degree in watching children's movies. During a recent intensive my son, Liam, and daughter, Tayla, watched *The Incredibles* with astonishing regularity. During their demanding training Liam lost himself in the story (like all good stories) and experienced a deep connection with the young character Dash.

For those of you who don't have a PhD in *The Incredibles*, Dash has the secret power of running like lightning. Liam watched the movie, jumped from the ground with both feet in the air and shouted, "I am Dash." Then he hurled his three-year-old body through the house with amazing sound effects and blistering speed, shouting, "I have the secret power of speed."

Unfortunately, Liam would forget his name. He would do his morning routine, go to school and totally forget his Dash identity. One late afternoon he approached me and asked, "Daddy, what is my name again?" I looked at him and said, "Liam, your name is Dash." As I reminded him he smiled and jumped into the air and ran down the hallway.

Remembering his identity activated his limbs. He knew his name and could then live into his "secret power." Liam teaches me to remember my identity. Jesus reveals to us our new names. I am Tom, a beloved child of God with the secret power of love.

In the formational naked journey we can easily forget our names. This identity amnesia leads to engaging with the discipline of formation or training without the relational foundation of God's accepting love. When we forget our identity as children of a loving God and train naked in order to earn God's acceptance, we develop spiritual cellulite. It is crucial to grasp that we train naked in the gymnasium of God's unconditional love.

In almost all of his letters the apostle Paul spends the first half reminding the congregations who they are (you are Dash/beloved) and then challenges them to move into different rhythms (training naked). We train naked from our identity as beloved children of God.

The classic word to explain God's unconditional love is *grace*. Imagine with me that the gymnasium of God is grace-filled. It is all grace. Unfortunately this rich and textured word has been reduced and flattened to describe only the forgiveness of sins. In this flattened state *grace* becomes the operative word for God's forgiveness. Grace as forgiveness is already "amazing grace," but that is not all there is to grace.

I sometimes ask church groups if Jesus needed grace. The temperature in the room usually rises. I see how people struggle with the question. Many of them process it in the following way: "We need grace to save us from sin. Jesus never sinned so he surely didn't need grace." But then they tap into all their experiences as pastors and teachers asking trick questions. A long, pregnant pause follows.

Did Jesus need grace?

In Luke we read that Jesus grew in grace and favor with God and humanity (Luke 2:40). Jesus didn't sin, so we can safely say that grace is more than just the forgiveness of sins. If I think of grace only as God's salvation coming to me as unearned favor, then I will not know how to live in grace in other areas of my life. Many people place grace in opposition to works. This thinking paralyzes many Christians and eliminates the effort to train naked. Dallas Willard notes that "grace is opposed to earning" but that "grace is not opposed to effort."[3] We are saved by grace from our sins, but we are then empowered by grace to train naked and grow in godliness.

The apostle Peter commands us to grow in the grace of God (2 Peter 3:18). But what does that mean? If we only think of grace as a saving and forgiving word, then we might think that to grow in the grace of God we have to sin more so that God can forgive us more. But that is not the case. Paul refuted this clearly when he asked, "What then are we to say? Should we continue in sin in order that grace may abound?" (Romans 6:1 NRSV). The question is rhetorical; we don't accumulate God's grace in this way!

I find Eugene Peterson's paraphrase of Romans 6 helpful.

So what do we do? Keep on sinning so God can keep on forgiving? I should hope not! If we've left the country where sin is sovereign, how can we still live in our old house there? Or didn't you realize we packed up and left there for good? That is what happened in baptism. When we went under the water, we left the old country of sin behind; when we came up out of the water, we entered into the new country of grace—a new life in a new land! That's what baptism into the life of Jesus means. (Romans 6:1-3)

I love this image of a new country. The new country of grace is the place where we are forgiven and empowered in order to live a new life. Grace forgives but also empowers. In the church as a grace-filled gymnasium we experience grace as forgiveness and empowerment. Grace gives a new name (Dash), and grace empowers us to train naked. Dallas Willard states this beautifully:

If you would really like to be into consuming grace, just lead a holy life. The true saint burns grace like a 747 burns fuel on takeoff. Become the kind of person who routinely does what Jesus did and said. You will consume much more grace by leading a holy life than you will by sinning, because every holy act you do will have to be upheld by the grace of God.[4]

As we train naked we stand firm on our God-given identity. Jesus died for our sins and gave us this grace. We are children of God (John 1:12). We embrace grace as forgiveness plus the power that enables us to do what we cannot do on our own.[5] Raw spirituality grows in grace—the foundational grace of forgiveness and the grace of training toward obedience. As we exercise in this grace-filled gymnasium we are forgiven and empowered to become naked or, in an edgy idiom, remove our butt skins.

NAKED: REMOVING OUR BUTT SKINS

Nakedness suggests openness and intimacy. It implies rawness. Rawness is the opposite of plastic and polished. I think this is one of the reasons why the biblical narrative starts with two people hanging around naked with God and each other—it indicates a life in the open, undisguised.

This rawness, "naked, and . . . not ashamed" (Genesis 2:25 NRSV), is the first thing lost when sin enters the story. As we are faced with our raw nakedness we are also tempted to hide. This hiding hinders growth because it separates us from a relationship with God and other people.

During the first four years of Claypot we rediscovered Jesus. We studied Matthew, Mark, Luke and John, and the Jesus we encountered in those narratives wooed and challenged us. He invited us to not only believe in but also to follow him. His grace of forgiveness was complemented by the gracious invitation to follow. Jesus lured us and shocked us. He invited and exposed us. Jesus invited us to become naked:

> Indeed, the word of God is living and active, sharper than any two-edged sword, piercing until it divides soul from spirit, joints from marrow; it is able to judge the thoughts and intentions of the heart. And before him no creature is hidden, but all are naked and laid bare to the eyes of the one to whom we must render an account. (Hebrews 4:12-13 NRSV)

The way we dealt with this loving exposure reminded me of school. When I went to school, teachers still used corporal punishment as discipline, usually with a stick. The maximum penalty was six strikes. Some of us removed the inner tubing of a bicycle wheel, cut a circle out of it, and then punched some holes in the tube. We concealed it under our pants for some extra protection. This was called a *gatvel* in Afrikaans (a literal translation is "butt skin"). The holes would muffle the sound of the tubing and minimize the pain—woe to those who were caught wearing it!

Imagine my surprise when I discovered that Kierkegaard used this image in his writings. He said that all of us have become accustomed to facing the reality of Jesus with a "butt skin." He writes,

Can't we be honest for once! We have become such experts at cunningly shoving one layer after another, one interpretation after another, between the Word and our lives (like a boy putting padding under his pants when he is about to get a spanking). We then allow this preoccupation to swell to such profundity that we never come to look at our lives in the mirror. All this interpreting and re-interpreting is but a defense against God's Word. It is all too easy to understand the requirements contained in God's Word ("Give all your goods to the poor." "If anyone strikes you on the right cheek, turn the left." "Count it sheer joy when you meet various temptations" etc.). The most ignorant, poor creature cannot honestly deny being able to understand God's requirements. But it is tough on the flesh to *will* to understand it and to then act accordingly. Herein lies the problem. It is not a question of interpretation, but action.[6]

Kierkegaard focuses on God's act of correcting (spanking with the stick) and our inability to face the discipline (the butt skin). As we discover Jesus, we recover an image of a loving God that disciplines us (see chap. 2). This disciplining leads to a life of training or discipleship. Discipleship without discipline or training is impossible. The Hebrew letter states,

> God is educating you; that's why you must never drop out. He's treating you as dear children. This trouble you're in isn't punishment; it's *training*, the normal experience of children. Only irresponsible parents leave children to fend for themselves. Would you prefer an irresponsible God? We respect our own parents for training and not spoiling us, so why not embrace God's training so we can truly *live*? While we were children, our parents did what *seemed* best to them. But God is doing what *is* best for us, training us to live God's holy best. (Hebrews 12:7-10)

As we encountered Jesus in the Gospels, we had to admit that we had many postmodern butt skins protecting us from his call to action and invitations to life (and we still do). We were confronted with the fact that we were raw recruits in desperate need of a new kind of spirituality.

Stanis, our worship leader, was one of the people who pointed out our butt skins. He showed us how we were making use of dualistic tactics to get away from obeying what Jesus called us to do. Here's what happened.

We were singing one Sunday; it was one of those magnificent moments when we felt God's presence. We sang enthusiastically, the kind of singing when we secretly like the way our singing sounds. (Maybe it is only me engaging in vanity like this.) The song extolled Jesus, and we declared, "we raise our hands to you."

The decibels were raised, but our hands weren't.

Stanis challenged us to create true synchronicity between the words "we raise our hands" and our bodies. "I know what some of you are thinking while you're singing this song," he said. "You think that you're not going to raise your hands right now, but that Jesus knows that 'deep in your heart' you are raising your hands."

Stanis confronted our butt-skin Christianity wherein we follow Jesus "deep in our hearts" without any kind of movement with our bodies. The next song we sang that day had the words, "You let me lie down in green pastures." Laughingly, Stanis sang the song lying down. We got his point.

Synchronicity between heart, mind and body is crucial in the development of a raw spirituality. The training-naked journey takes place in the gymnasium of grace; this gives us the confidence to acknowledge our butt skins and become naked.

Training naked is not only corporate but also a personal journey, and means that I learn how to break through my defense mechanisms. Psychologists have taught us that we use defense mechanisms to protect ourselves against challenges and growth. In fact, I just employed one in the previous sentence. Can you spot my defense mechanism?

I used the defense mechanism of not speaking for myself. By using "we" language we sometimes hide from the truth. Did you see what I did there, again? Let me try that again. By using "we" language I sometimes hide from the truth. If I am going to engage in raw spirituality I will have to work on owning my own naked rawness and stop hiding in the collective. Have you noticed how easy it is to hide? Here are a few typical phrases that illustrate how we hide (oops, I did it again):

- "You know, people battle with racism."
- "You know, you just don't have enough time to train in godliness."
- "People battle with reaching out."
- "A person is just too tired to build friendships."
- "You know, we are just so focused on becoming rich."

In order to grow I will have to bust the defense mechanisms I use. In Christian history this is called confession. I need help with this. That is why I will have to invite some of my good friends to help me, and I need to become part of a church that makes regular confession part of its worship. I recently asked a friend to help me when I use defense mechanisms. We had a conversation in which I said, "You know, you just don't feel motivated to read the Bible." To which my friend responded, "I am very motivated at the moment, so I don't think you can speak for me." We laughed and I changed the sentence to an "I" statement.

As I said, *we* all battle with defense mechanisms. . . . Let me try that again, *I* battle with defense mechanisms.

Training naked takes place in the gymnasium of God's grace. This helps me to remove my butt skins and thereby become naked. Then I am able to train or, to use a Jesus phrase, "change and become like children" (Matthew 18:3 NRSV).

TRAINING: BECOMING LIKE CHILDREN AGAIN

In 2000 Lollie and I moved to the United States from our native country, South Africa. It was like switching kingdoms. We had to re-learn some of the basic everyday reflexes we took for granted. Driving was one of the responses that had to be retrained. In South Africa we drive on the "right" side of the road, which is the left-hand side.

After several years of driving in South Africa on the left it became second nature to us. So when we moved to the States we had to become accustomed to driving on the "wrong" side of the road, which is the right-hand side. In order to become an active part of the kingdom of the United States we had to change and become like children, otherwise we would not be able to live in the States. It took some serious unlearning to rewire what was second nature to us. It was a form of conversion.

In the beginning it was tough because we felt that we were regressing by driving on the "wrong" side of the road. But after a few weeks driving on the right-hand side of the road, it felt comfortable and even "right." After three years of driving on the right-hand side of the road, it was quite an adjustment to drive in South Africa on the left-hand side of the road, because it didn't feel right.

Entering the United States was like entering a new kingdom where we had to learn the new rhythms of this kingdom. In terms of driving we had to change and become like children again. We even had to retake the exams with American sixteen-year-olds and do the driving test again. Jesus notes, "I'm telling you, once and for all, that unless you return to square one and start over like children, you're not even going to get a look at the kingdom, let alone get in" (Matthew 18:3).

When Jesus uses kingdom language it is not just a synonym for heaven. God's kingdom is the reality where what God wants to happen happens. Or to quote Dallas Willard, "The kingdom of God is the range of God's effective will, where what God wants done is done."[7] We are invited to now live within the wild adventurous kingdom of our loving Father in an intimate relationship with Jesus empowered by the Spirit. This is what we train for.

Like our move to the United States, living in the kingdom of God means that we change and become like children again. We unlearn and relearn. Training naked is adopting anew the mind of a child.

Missiologist Alan Kreider refers to this unlearning process in a beautiful way when he describes discipleship in the early church. He writes that when new converts to Christianity entered the flock, they had to learn new reflexes. This process was called catechism and could take up to three years. During the catechism the catechumen (person going through the catechism) had to change what Kreider calls their "folkways." He explains folkways:

> I use this term [folkways] rather than "ethics" or "morality" because it has to do with the ways of a people which are often assumed rather than consciously thought out; they are habitual, even reflexive. The pagans undergoing catechism needed to be *rehabituated* so that they would react to situations of tension and difficulty in a distinctive way, not like pagans, but like members of a Christian community, and ideally like Jesus. At the heart of

the imparting of folkways, as Origen pointed out, was imitation: hence the importance of the life example on the part of catechists and sponsors alike.[8]

As we follow Jesus we enter a process of learning new reflexes or folkways that reflect the goodness of the triune God. The foundation of this process is to be born from above (John 3:3). We become children of God. Then we become like children and train into the new kingdom reality. When we accept Jesus' gift of being born again, we become like children embarking on a journey where we learn a whole new way of being human. Raw spirituality engages with a lifelong process of learning; this is the excitement of training naked.

When we planted the church in South Africa, most of us were newlyweds or single. Marnis Antonites was the first of a holy avalanche of children born into our community. Because Marnis was the eldest of our holy posse, we got to watch him closely.

As a church family we decided that we were going to welcome these children in our midst and that all members were responsible for them. This meant that everyone got an opportunity to be with the children during the Sunday service. This was hard for many, especially those who weren't used to children. For some of them these few hours spent with little ones became the only contact with God's unique teachers. Time and again we heard beautiful stories of how the children taught the adults some beautiful lessons.

As a part of our relearning what it means to follow Jesus we purposefully decided not to buy a church building. We met in a community hall. This theological decision merged our story with the larger community who met there for all kinds of activities, ranging from pottery classes to yoga and even belly dancing. The community hall was protected by a security guard who sat in a small hut to the side of the parking lot. Every Sunday Marnis would walk up to the security guard and engage in conversation with him. In Marnis's eyes the security guard was not just a nameless person merged with his function. Marnis saw him as a person—Ronald.

When our daughter, Tayla, was born, we observed the same in her. She was able to notice and see in ways that we had lost. I still remember one day when we were at the supermarket. As we were paying at the checkout we greeted the clerk. Tayla tugged on my trousers and in her familiar one-word sentences asked me, "Name?" She wanted to engage with the clerk not just as a clerk, a function, but also importantly as someone with a story.

As we observe children, we find that they have an insatiable curiosity. Recent research showed that a four-year-old girl asks 390 questions per day, averaging a question every 1 minute, 56 seconds of her waking day.[9] As we train naked, we also learn how to quest with good questions. We are discovering the amazing gift of asking each other good questions. This is an essential part of raw spirituality.

Doing life with children is not always romantic; I am intimately aware that they also become habituated into destructive folkways. But still. We can learn something about and from children by studying them closely. Children help us to re-reflex.

Gary Thomas writes that

> we live in the midst of holy teachers. Sometimes they spit up on themselves or on us. Sometimes they throw tantrums. Sometimes they cuddle us and kiss us and love us. In the good and the bad they mold our hearts, shape our souls, and invite us to experience God in newer and deeper ways.[10]

Being "born again" and "changing and becoming like children" are prerequisites for growth. Know-it-alls cannot grow. Jesus once stated, "I thank you, Father, Lord of heaven and earth, because you have hidden these things from the wise and the intelligent and have revealed them to infants" (Matthew 11:25 NRSV).

Training naked takes place in the grace-filled gymnasium of God. This grace brings forgiveness and empowerment. As beloved children we learn new rhythms that help us to live within God's kingdom, making the world a better place.

In chapter two we will kick-start our journey with our God pictures.

Training Naked

FOR REFLECTION AND DISCUSSION

First, read through all these questions and explore the ones that intrigue you. Journal some of your answers. When you gather with your companions, discuss your responses.

1. How would you describe grace in your life?

2. In which parts of your life would you like to be "born again" or "become like a child"?

3. Which new reflexes are you currently learning?

4. Which questions are you currently wrestling with?

5. What are some of your butt skins?

INDIVIDUAL EXERCISE

During this week take some time to reflect on your day. Attempt at least three reflection times. During the evening, rewind the day in your head and pray through the different scenes. Here are some questions that might help you. If you are a journaling type of person, write down your reflections.

1. Which parts of your day were joyful?

2. When did you experience sadness or grief?

3. What would you do differently?

4. What did you hear?

5. Is there something you feel led toward?

GROUP EXERCISE

Brainstorm together on how your group can become a gymnasium of grace. Think of the three aspects discussed in this chapter: grace, removing butt skins (becoming naked) and training (becoming like children). Write down some practical steps.

TWO

Jesus with a Six-Pack

Jesus interprets God in the language of a human life.

HANS URS VON BALTHASAR

*The acid test for any theology is this: Is the God presented
one that can be loved, heart, soul, mind, and strength?
If the thoughtful, honest answer is "Not really,"
then we need to look elsewhere or deeper.*

DALLAS WILLARD

One of my good friends in the United States is Tom Hook. One day
while Tom was in the gymnasium, a pastor of one of the local churches
approached him with a strange request. "Would you be Jesus in our
Easter play?" Tom didn't know the pastor at all and was totally per-
plexed by the request. He asked the pastor why he wanted him to be
Jesus in their play. The pastor explained that he asked Tom for two
reasons. First, Tom was handsome. His features reminded this pastor
of Jesus. Second, Tom had a six-pack. This pastor wanted a Jesus with
a six-pack. After hearing these two reasons Tom declined.

Tom's gym partner then told him a remarkable story. He visited a large church that had a spectacular Easter production. The quality of the performance was so important to this church that they hired some of the country's best actors. This specific year Jesus was not a Christian but an actor.

The production went well up to the point where the Jesus who was not a Christian hung on the cross. They came to the scene where the soldier pierced Jesus' side. The problem was that the soldier took his job very seriously and instead of doing a fake stabbing he actually pierced Jesus' skin.

What happened next shocked everyone in the auditorium. The actor playing Jesus, who was strapped with one of those funky microphones seen on MTV, looked at the soldier and exclaimed, "When I get off this cross I am going to kick your butt."

Imagine explaining this scene to your impressionable child. But this was not the end!

The church had a contingency plan in place if something happened to their first choice of Jesus. They had a backup Jesus. Kick-your-butt Jesus was replaced. Now, in their production they combined the crucifixion and the ascension. Using a trolley system, they hoisted backup Jesus into the air as he ascended to heaven. What they didn't account for was that backup Jesus was heavier than Jesus who was not a Christian. Halfway to heaven the trolley snapped and backup Jesus fell to the ground, breaking both legs.

I am sure this church still deals with children who were scarred during this production. How do you reconcile this account with the text that reads, "None of his bones shall be broken" (John 19:36 NRSV)?

All of us paint mental pictures of Jesus. Our engagement with raw spirituality starts with our God pictures.

The number one is in the middle of the rhythm of life (see fig. 2.1). It reminds us to live in and from God as the center of our lives. With the number one symbol we ask the question, What is my current picture of God? We get the number one symbol from Mark 12:28-31. A man asks Jesus, "Which is most important of all the commandments?" Jesus responds with a remix of Deuteronomy 6:4-5 and Leviticus 19:18.

Figure 2.1

Jesus said, "The first in importance is, 'Listen, Israel: The Lord your God is one; so love the Lord God with all your passion and prayer and intelligence and energy.' And here is the second: 'Love others as well as you love yourself.' There is no other commandment that ranks with these."

The Deuteronomy passage is known as the *Shema*, which is the Hebrew word for "listen." Drawing healthy pictures of God takes place when we pay attention to Jesus. When we listen to Jesus we develop healthy pictures of the one God. In the book of Hebrews we read, "This Son perfectly mirrors God, and is stamped with God's nature. He holds everything together by what he says—powerful words!" (Hebrews 1:3).

The Gospel writings engage us with the life, death and resurrection of Jesus. Scripture is the crucial acoustic space for the church's listening. In the middle of three of the four Gospels (Matthew 16:13-20; Mark 8:27-30; Luke 9:18-21) we find the same telling of what we might call Jesus' master drawing class. Here is what happened.

When Jesus arrived in the villages of Caesarea Philippi, he asked his disciples, "What are people saying about who the Son of Man is?"

They replied, "Some think he is John the Baptizer, some say Elijah, some Jeremiah or one of the other prophets."

He pressed them, "And how about you? Who do you say I am?"

Simon Peter said, "You're the Christ, the Messiah, the Son of the living God."

Jesus came back, "God bless you, Simon, son of Jonah! You didn't get that answer out of books or from teachers. My Father in heaven, God himself, let you in on this secret of who I really am." (Matthew 16:13-17)

Jesus' master class consists of three parts. The first part explores the place where we paint. The second part explores pictures other people draw and is captured in the question "Who do the people say that I am?" The third part is the personal question "Who do you say that I am?"

THE PLACE(S) WHERE WE PAINT

When I was a kid, my mother and father would warn me about certain places. I had to stay away from these places because people who my parents described as unsavory hung out there. My dad would say, "If I ever find you at this place, you will regret it." I got the message.

As we read the Bible we have to remind ourselves that geographical information within the text helps us to understand the context. In Matthew 16:13 we read that Jesus goes to Caesarea Philippi. In Galilee, where Jesus grew up, Jewish children were also warned. Their parents warned them against the pagans and their practices. One of their unsavory places was Caesarea Philippi. Good Jewish children did not venture there.

Caesarea Philippi was originally a place of worship for the god Pan, called Paneas. In Jesus' lifetime Herod the Great's son Philip used the temple there for the worship of the emperor. The name of the city was a tribute to himself and to the Roman Caesar. Herod's son inherited some serious ego issues from his dad, Herod the Great.

A cave at Caesarea Philippi became the center of pagan sacrifices to Pan. During springtime a stream would flow from within the cave, which was known as the gates of Hades. Here people would make offerings to the gods.

Jesus chose this hostile place to ask the twin questions "Who do the people say I am?" and "Who do you say I am?" Jesus conducted a Bible study in a no-go zone. In Jesus' teaching method we find important values: the places we are in and the people we are with influence greatly the God pictures we draw.

Answering the questions "Who do the people say I am?" and "Who do you say I am?" will vary according to the context they are asked in. The responses of comfortable suburban people in an air-conditioned building will be different than those at the edge of the city in a squatter camp with scant housing and no heating. A raw spirituality develops as we paint Christ pictures in diverse places with people that challenge our worldview and affluence.

During apartheid, in privileged "whites only" places, people of sameness in the white church drew distorted pictures of Jesus. These positions of affluence and superiority led to toxic God pictures that favored people with a certain skin color.

In order to paint new pictures we are invited to journey to Caesarea Philippi. This will lead to unique and contextual paintings of Jesus. My experience as a rich suburban pastor is that the suburban church stands in danger of developing our Christology (the fancy word for our Jesus pictures) in botanical gardens, air-conditioned rooms and silent-retreat centers. However, Jesus' master class location reminds us that we are also invited to paint in wildernesses, places of desolation, inner cities and no-go zones. We are invited to our own versions of Caesarea Philippi.

WHO DO THE PEOPLE SAY I AM?

The second part of Jesus' master class explores the culture's Jesus pictures. I love asking people what they think of Jesus. Everyone has an opinion, and most people like to share it. In Jesus' time the pictures people had of him were filled with the heroes of the Old Testament, the prophets: Elijah and Jeremiah and Jesus' contemporary John the

Baptist. When I ask people who Jesus is, I hardly ever get those answers. The following are some of the answers I get.

Quite a few people have a picture of Jesus that I have come to call the "Jesus with the flower in the ear." This Jesus is irenic and wants everything to be okay. He is a loving and peaceful person that everyone likes but suspects is not totally in touch with reality. This "Jesus with the flower in the ear" occasionally lifts his hands to give the peace sign. He is harmless and nice. He is the kind of person you take to your grandmother for high tea. Closely related to this image is the "Lovely Jesus." In my first language, Afrikaans, a lot of children's first prayers are addressed to "Liewe Jesus." It brings to mind a Jesus that is still a child; he is as sweet and innocent, a little baby—petite Jesus.

The cinema helps us answer the question "Who do the people say I am?" Whenever I go to the cinema or watch movies at home, I listen to the different answers to Jesus' question. In the movie *Talladega Nights*, Ricky Bobby (Will Ferrell) is portrayed praying grace to "baby Jesus" and a huge debate breaks out at the table when his wife tells him that it is "a bit odd and off-puttin' to pray to a baby." Ricky responds,

> I like the Christmas Jesus best and I'm sayin' grace. When you say grace you can say it to grown-up Jesus, or teenage Jesus, or bearded Jesus, or whoever you want . . . [continues praying] Dear tiny Jesus, with your golden fleece diapers, with your tiny little fat balled-up fist . . .

His father-in-law responds, "He was a man! He had a beard." To which Ricky retorts, "Look, I like the baby Jesus version the best. Do you hear me?"

At this point the rest of those seated at the table share their favorite pictures of Jesus:

"I like to picture Jesus in a tuxedo T-shirt, 'cos it says, like, I wanna be formal, but I'm here to party too. I like to party, so I like my Jesus to party."

"I like to picture Jesus as a ninja fighting off evil samurai."

"I like to think of Jesus, like, with giant eagle's wings, and singin' lead vocals for Lynyrd Skynyrd with, like, a angel band, and I'm in the front row, and I'm hammered drunk."[1]

In the movie *Paul*, an extended critique is leveled at fundamental Christianity. Paul (an alien) liberates a young woman who is portrayed as being trapped by a certain picture of Jesus. In the movie she wears a T-shirt with a picture of Jesus with a handgun. Next to Jesus stands Darwin with his head blown off. The caption on the T-shirt reads, "Evolve this." The picture shows a violent Jesus with gangsta attitude; I call this the "Terminator Jesus." He, like Arnold Schwarzenegger, says, "I'll be back" and is a lot like the actor Jesus on the cross—"when I get off this cross I am going to kick your butt."

As Paul the alien liberates the girl from her religious trappings, she responds by enjoying her life through sex and drink. The implicit message of the movie *Paul* is that Jesus prohibits people from enjoying life, and all Christians fight against Darwinism.

Advertisements also contain answers to "Who do the people say I am?" A few years ago the Humanist Association in London ran an advertising campaign on London buses that said, "There probably is not a God so stop worrying and enjoy your life."[2] The campaign was launched after Ariane Sherine became angry when she noticed a set of Christian ads in a London bus with a website address which warned that people who reject God are condemned to spend all eternity to "torment in Hell." This offended her, so she started the bus campaign. Her picture is a non-God, or if there is a God, one that makes you worry and who makes life unenjoyable.

Art also answers the "Who do the people say I am?" question. One of the artists that fascinate me is Banksy. He is a graffiti artist. No one knows his true identity. He portrays Jesus hanging on a cross with Christmas shopping bags in his hands.[3] This image reflects on Jesus as a personal Savior in a very consumerist sense. This is what happens when Christians admire and accept Jesus but don't follow him. The Dane Søren Kierkegaard made the distinction between admirers and followers of Jesus. When we admire Jesus we so easily see him in the same category as shopping. Jesus becomes a product that I consume, and church becomes the shopping mall.

Our culture is awash with different God pictures. The exciting adventure of raw spirituality is to become aware of these pictures and become people who paint beautiful pictures of God in the Spirit of Jesus. I think this is why Jesus taught us to pray "hallowed be your name" (Matthew 6:9 NRSV), which can be paraphrased "help us to draw healing pictures of you."

To the culture(s) we find ourselves in, followers of Jesus draw pictures of God through our lives. With God's help within God's diverse body we bring healing to distorted paintings.

WHO DO YOU SAY I AM?

Jesus moves his disciples toward the more personal question "Who do you say I am?" We move from what the culture says about Jesus to our own pictures of Jesus. To answer Jesus' question I am using four images that I have learned from Richard Foster and Renovaré.

Jesus as Savior. One of my initial pictures of Jesus is Savior. Jesus died on the cross for me so I can go to heaven. This is the picture that moved me toward Jesus. I became thoroughly convinced of my own sinfulness on the one hand and God's unconditional love and grace on the other. As a seventeen-year-old I "accepted Jesus as my personal Savior."

For many years this was my only image of Jesus. I reduced the whole biblical narrative to this one drawing of Jesus. The Bible became an extended message saying "Jesus saved you." Coming to Jesus was totally informed by wanting to be forgiven. Jesus' saving action was limited to him saving me from my individual sins. Jesus was really good at saving me from my sins—it was a picture of Jesus on the cross.

I had a good sense of what Jesus saved me from but not what he saved me toward (except for heaven one day). In order to be saved the church reminded me of my sinfulness. The sins that Jesus saved me from were evils like lying, cussing, smoking and other external acts of impiety.

At this stage of my journey I had no sense of structural sins like apartheid. It was all about me: my own individual sins and my personal relationship with God. Many years later I had a Caesarea Philippi experience when I read a statement by the young activist Steve Biko, a man who was killed by the apartheid regime in 1977:

> The Church and its operation in modern-day South Africa has therefore to be looked at in terms of the way it was introduced in this country. Even at this late stage, one notes the appalling irrelevance of the interpretation given to the Scriptures. In a country teeming with injustice and fanatically committed to the practice of oppression, intolerance and blatant cruelty because of racial bigotry; in a country where all black people are made to feel the unwanted step-children of a God whose presence they cannot feel; in a country where father and son, mother and daughter alike develop daily into neurotics through sheer inability to relate the present to the future because of a completely engulfing sense of destitution, the Church further adds to their insecurity by its inward-directed definition of the concept of sin and its encouragement of the "mea culpa" attitude.[4]

Biko challenges the narrowness of a personal Jesus as Savior. Now let me be clear: I still believe that Jesus saves me from my sins, but I also believe that he saves us from being oppressors and oppressed, and that sin includes more than just my own personal sins—it also touches on the ways I sin structurally—it includes the sin of the world.

This issue is a crucial part of what followers of Jesus will have to grapple with in our ever-connecting globalized world. The coffee I drink, T-shirts I wear, music I listen to and food I eat are all connected.

By consumption I might be promoting someone's oppression in another part of the world. Jesus also saves from that. Salvation also has implications for these forms of structural sin.

Over the years my concept of salvation has become more comprehensive and holistic to include more of my life, every part, not just salvation for the afterlife but also for my life before death. Amazing grace how sweet the sound that saved a wretch like me.

Jesus as a brilliant intellectual teacher. We tend to admire someone who is good at something. When Steve Jobs passed away, millions of people commented on his life and legacy. He was good at several things. It is a normal part of life; we follow people who we reckon are good at something.

One day I experimented on my Facebook and Twitter accounts. I asked the question, "What is Jesus good at?" The responses were interesting. The number one response was, "Jesus is good at saving me," and the second was "Jesus is good at being Jesus." Whenever I got the second response I gently pushed people to probe a bit further. But most people stayed with the answer of "Jesus is good at being Jesus." I understand this ontological answer, but I don't think that it is helpful. Jesus is kept in a foggy haze where we can't really say what he is good at.

At the end of Matthew Jesus calls his followers to make disciples and states, "All authority in heaven and on earth has been given to me" (Matthew 28:18 NRSV).

Our culture still asks questions about authority; we want to know "Who is the authority in this arena?" It is interesting that Jesus says *all* authority has been given to him. That includes everything. Jesus is the authority on all areas of life: medicine, education, economics, psychology, politics, parenting and the list goes on. He is good at all those things. Whenever I explore this with people, I sense them tense up. Some people feel uncomfortable to place Jesus in the realm of real life. For a long while this was one of my distorted drawings of Jesus; he was the authority for the "spiritual life" but not the "real life."

In addition to Savior Jesus, we engage smart Jesus. I want to emphasize again, Jesus is Savior but he is also more than Savior. He is also Teacher. If Jesus is "The authority" then he must be intelligent. But do we think of Jesus as the smartest person who ever lived? If I only think he was good at saving my soul in order to go to heaven, why would I want to follow him in my "real life"?

Think about it, Jesus knew how to influence weather patterns through his physical presence—I don't know someone who has this kind of authority. Jesus knew how to change water into wine and dead cells into living cells. I don't know anyone else like that. Dallas Willard shares how he asks university students to list the smartest people who ever lived. Jesus hardly ever makes the list.[5]

If we follow Jesus as Teacher, then we must acknowledge that he is good at teaching and has a sense of what he is talking about. If we don't think Jesus is brilliant, we will relegate his teachings into a compartmentalized spiritual aspect of our lives that we think is not "in touch with reality."

When I realize Jesus' brilliance, I will follow his teachings as the "Author of life" (Acts 3:15 NRSV) and the one who invites me into a life of fullness (John 10:10). This will turn some of the so-called authorities and their claims on their head.

Jesus as Lord to be obeyed. In one of Jesus' most famous sermons he asks arrestingly, "Why do you call me 'Lord, Lord,' and do not do what I tell you?" (Luke 6:46 NRSV). Jesus addresses another picture here: Lord. Painting the Lord picture implies movement toward obedience. At the end of Matthew when Jesus says all authority has been given to him, he challenges his disciples to teach the people to "obey everything that I have commanded you" (Matthew 28:20 NRSV). In our information-obsessed world we might read it as "teaching them to know everything I have commanded you."

The word *lord* is not a particularly religious word. It comes from the domain of slavery as in "a lord that commands his slave." The word implies that someone is above you and has the authority to command you.

In the television series *Downton Abbey* the relationships of lords and servants are depicted. If there is a lord, then there is a servant. In the television series some lords are gracious; others are not. If you have an overbearing master who exploits others, then it will be hard to serve. But if the lord you are serving is also your Savior and Teacher, then the way you serve will surely change.

It is nonsensical to call Jesus Lord if I don't believe he has authority (or actually is the authority), and it will also be unusual if I don't think his authority means that something has to be changed or acted out in my actual life. In other words, if I accept Jesus as Savior, I am also invited to engage with him as Teacher. When I live out his teachings or obey his commands, I get to know Jesus as my Lord. This has implications for life after death and life before death. Paul says it like this: "For if while we were enemies, we were reconciled to God through the death of his Son, much more surely, having been reconciled, will we be saved by his life" (Romans 5:10 NRSV).

Now, let me be honest. As a child of the postmodern age I have difficulty with the image of Jesus as Lord. I have a natural suspicion of people placed over me, and I battle to think of myself as a slave (or the softer word *servant*).

What complicates this further is that I am used to all kinds of options. I am a child of the multiple-choice generation. When a worship leader leads the congregation, she or he gives options; people are invited to sit, stand, lie down or do whatever they want. I like options that cater to different personalities. But what will happen if the choices I make always cater to my specific individualistic or even our group's homogeneous tastes?

There is no getting away from Jesus as Lord. If we are going to rid ourselves from a flabby image of Jesus, we will have to engage with the concept of his lordship in whose name "every knee will bow" and "tongue confess" (Philippians 2). I am not naturally a bow-before-someone type of guy. This is why I need Jesus as Savior. His grace forgives and empowers me.

Bowing becomes easier as I engage in the crucial journey to discovering the brilliance of Jesus. If I truly believe that he is intelligent and can speak into my reality, then I can actually put his brilliant teachings into practice and listen to his invitations to "follow me" and "come to me." Jesus becomes Lord in my life. Every month I ask myself the difficult questions, Where have I followed Jesus as Lord? Where did I obey Jesus? Growth in obedience is a crucial part of being a disciple of Jesus.

Jesus as friend. In the Gospel of John there is an immensely intimate scene. It is the last time Jesus and his disciples hang out before the crucifixion. He prepares them for the tumultuous times ahead. Jesus washes their feet, shares an intimate meal with singing and prayers, and speaks words of comfort and blessing. John 13–17 gives us a seat at the table where we can watch Jesus and his interaction with his disciples. During the intimate conversation Jesus uses two of the images we have already explored. He says to his disciples,

> You call me Teacher and Lord—and you are right, for that is what I am. So if I, your Lord and Teacher, have washed your feet, you also ought to wash one another's feet. For I have set you an example, that you also should do as I have done to you. Very truly, I tell you, servants are not greater than their master, nor are messengers greater than the one who sent them. If you know these things, you are blessed if you do them. (John 13:13-17 NRSV)

Here is another one of those neglected beatitudes: "If you know these things, blessed are you if you do them." In an information-overload culture we can easily mistake knowing for doing. In fact, I think this is one of the biggest mistakes we Google-loving people make. We mistake knowing for doing, and spiritual formation becomes reduced to interesting information (like sociohistoric background).

Notice how Jesus tells his disciples that they already drew pictures of him as Teacher and as Lord, and he now invites them, to borrow a Nike slogan, to just do it!

Later in this beautiful and intimate scene that takes place in the Upper Room, Jesus tells his disciples,

> This is my commandment, that you love one another as I have loved you. No one has greater love than this, to lay down one's life for one's friends. You are my friends if you do what I command you. I do not call you servants any longer, because the servant does not know what the master is doing; but I have called you friends, because I have made known to you every-thing that I have heard from my Father. (John 15:12-15 NRSV)

Jesus ties together beautifully the different images that we have ex-plored. He invites them into a friendship where they do whatever Jesus commands them. The "if" as in "if you do what I command" might confront us a bit, but I think it makes perfect sense.

When I experience Jesus as Savior, he gracefully forgives my sin and gracefully empowers me to live in a new life. I then take him to be my authority. Jesus shows me what the "master is doing." We are in on the exciting dream God has for his world, even before we die! As disciples we learn to obey Jesus as the Master or Lord, and then Jesus says that he views us as more than lowly servants. We become his friends. This is a very freeing image; we can easily follow Jesus in such a way that it is all about sacrifice and grit and hard work, and then we miss the joy of walking with Jesus as a friend.

If we get stuck with the images of Jesus as Teacher and Lord, the impact on our life with God can become oppressive. This makes me grind my teeth because it produces an "I am sacrificing for Jesus" kind of spirituality. This is the temptation of the activists.

The drawings of Jesus as Teacher and Lord need the beautiful hues of Jesus as Savior and Friend. Paul understood this beautiful mix when he called himself a "coworker" with Jesus (1 Corinthians 3:9 NIV).

On the other hand some of us have only two drawings of Jesus; we avoid the Lord image, skipping the "if you do what I command you" part. We merge the images of Jesus as Savior and Jesus as Friend without mixing in the images of Teacher and Lord. This is a temptation of the contemplative. It becomes an inward-focused life that revels in Jesus as Savior and Friend but misses the exciting adventure of getting in on what the Master is doing. This is epitomized by a famous devotional technique based on the first part of a verse in the Psalms,

> Be still and know that I am God
> Be still and know that I am
> Be still and know
> Be still
> Be

I appreciate this movement, but there is a second part to the verse: "I will be exalted among the nations" (Psalm 46:10 NIV). As we inwardly engage with our Savior and Friend, we outwardly adventure toward the interrupting exaltation of God as Teacher and Lord in the everyday lives of our cultures. This brings the contemplative and activist journeys together. It shows people that we are living hopeful lives and leads them to ask why.

Much of our consumer culture comprises people who substitute other people's authority for Jesus' authority in their lives. In the week-to-week journeys these authorities become our lords in areas of economics, parenting, relationships and other realms of life. Then on a Sunday for an hour we sing about Jesus as Savior and imagine him as our best friend, but his teachings and lordship are absent in the rest of our lives.

This tragedy of the absence of Jesus' authority and lordship merges well with our idea of God as a vending machine and church services as a shopping mall. So, we are invited to add the drawings of Jesus as Teacher and as Lord.

Next time when you sing worship songs notice the pictures that are drawn.

Jesus calls us his friends. Jesus calls you his friend. In our Facebook culture one can imagine the following scene. Have you ever sent someone a friend request that you thought was way out of your league? It might be to a celebrity or to someone you really respect. What does it feel like to send out the friend invitation hoping that the other person would accept? I feel exhilarated and vulnerable. Maybe the person will accept, but he or she may also decide to ignore me.

Now imagine receiving a friend request from someone that you respect, and you didn't initiate the friendship! Imagine sitting at your computer and suddenly getting a message saying that Bono wants to be your friend.

In Jesus' day there was no Facebook, but they also had certain relational dynamics. One was the relationship between a rabbi and his disciples. A rabbi would never send out a friend request to a would-be disciple; that was not how they rolled. A disciple had to initiate, and the relationship didn't have a friendship dynamic to it. All rabbis waited for would-be disciples to initiate, but there was one exception. Jesus sent out a friend request to the disciples. Here is what Jesus said:

> I'm no longer calling you servants because servants don't under-stand what their master is thinking and planning. No, I've named you friends because I've let you in on everything I've heard from the Father.
>
> "You didn't choose me, remember; I chose you, and put you in the world to bear fruit, fruit that won't spoil. As fruit bearers, whatever you ask the Father in relation to me, he gives you. (John 15:15-16)

Notice how Jesus reminds them that he initiated the friend request: "I chose you." Can you picture a Jesus that chose you? How does that make you feel? How do we respond to this?

In our Facebook world the term *friend* has been diluted. In the Facebook world a "friend" might be someone who can see your status updates, and that might be the only connection Facebook friends have. It can become pretty shallow. The friendship Jesus invites us into is more than that. Jesus invites us into "everything that I have heard from my Father"(John 15:15 NRSV). This friendship connects us to the heart of God!

But that is not all. Our friendship also has implications for the world. Spiritual formation that is not making the world better is a dead end and will turn in on itself and become toxic.

When my son, Liam, was four years old, I told him about Jesus and his disciples. He listened attentively and then reflected back what he heard (his mom is a psychologist so these skills are introduced early on). I found Liam's summary refreshing. He said to me, "So Jesus formed a gang doing good?"

I *like* that, to stay with the Facebook metaphor.

Jesus sends us a friend request and then invites us to join his group, a gang that bears fruit and does good to beautify this world.

To unpack this a bit further I want to share with you the way the Greeks (influenced by Aristotle) viewed friendships. According to Aristotle there are three kinds of friendships. The first describes people who become friends because the other person is *useful*. This is the kind of friendship that gets described as "networking" today. The other person is a resource. We even have whole business units set up to manage these kinds of relationships—HR, "human resources."

The second type of friendship can be described as relationships that are *pleasant*. I am your friend because I enjoy your company and you mine. We like each other. When we are together we have good times.

The third type of friendship brings *goodness*. When these friends come together they plan goodness for each other and the places where they live. They become conspirators of goodness and subvert the system with beauty. For Aristotle the last category is the purest form of friendship.

I find these types of friendship helpful in reflecting on my relationship with Jesus. I think when Jesus calls us his friends he has the third type in mind; he calls us to bear fruit in the world. The South African author David Bosch uses a beautiful metaphor to describe the kind of fruit we bear:

> We still live in the unredeemed world, but we may walk with our heads held high; we know that the kingdom is coming because it has already come. We live within the creative tension between the already and the not yet, forever moving closer to the orbit of the former. We Christians are an anachronism in this world: not anymore what we used to be, but not yet what we are destined to be. We are too early for heaven, yet too late for the world. We live on the borderline between the already and the not yet. We are a fragment of the world to come, God's colony in a human world, his experimental garden on earth. We are like crocuses in the snow, a sign of the world to come and at the same time a guarantee of its coming.[6]

Jesus sends us a friend request and invites us to join his group. We become a Jesus gang bearing fruit and beautifying this world. Our gang's charter flows from our collective pictures of Jesus. He is our Savior, Teacher, Lord and Friend.

Together we learn from Jesus how to draw God. The Holy Spirit takes our hands and helps us when we draw our pictures of Jesus. The drawing takes place individually but also corporately. The pictures are painted in intimate places *and* Caesarea Philippi zones. We compare our pictures with those painted in the Gospels. We continue to pray, "hallowed be your name" or "help us to paint healthy pictures of you."

Training Naked

FOR REFLECTION AND DISCUSSION

1. What is a Caesarea Philippi in your area?

2. Who is Jesus in your culture? A great exercise is to take your camera or notebook and walk through your culture with Jesus' question in mind. Ask people and investigate—it might open some interesting conversations for you!

3. Which of the four pictures of Jesus (Savior, Teacher, Lord, Friend) invites you at the moment? Why?

INDIVIDUAL EXERCISE

I want to invite you during this week to pray a simple prayer three times a day:

Holy Spirit, help me to draw healthy pictures of Jesus.

If you want you can also pray "hallowed be your name," which I paraphrase as "help us to draw healthy pictures of God."

Then choose any of the Gospels (Matthew, Mark, Luke, John) and start reading one of them. Note the different drawings of Jesus.

GROUP EXERCISE

Gather a group of friends to do a Jesus-style Bible study. Identify a Caesarea Philippi in your town or city. Make sure that you go as a group and then study Matthew 16:13-28. For a bonus experience invite someone that brings diversity to the group.

THREE

Got Power?

Spiritual commitments, if they are to be helpful, need to be translated into specific and concrete terms. Otherwise they remain pious-sounding and abstract concepts that mean little when it comes to the real business of everyday life.

TREVOR HUDSON

The more we train ourselves to spend time with God and him alone, the more we will discover that God is with us at all times and in all places.

HENRI NOUWEN

Have you noticed the people in coffee shops with the laptop bags? What do they look for when they enter a coffee shop? Amazing coffee *and* a power source and Wi-Fi! It is coffee shop suicide to build a store without giving patrons access to power and connectivity. In these days of smartphones, tablets and laptops we all need power for our gadgets. Everyday the liturgical question linked to our dependence on power is uttered all over the world between friends, spouses and family members: "Have you seen my charger?"

WHAT CHARGES YOU?

Without power most of us cannot function. In recent weeks a nearby town was without electricity for six days. Can you imagine six days without power? Take some time and think through your everyday experiences and make a list of all your power-dependent activities.

Figure 3.1

Our dependence on power is why one of the rhythms is represented by the symbol of a plug (see fig. 3.1). Everyday we plug in and charge our devices. The plug rhythm reminds us of the wonderful invitation God gives us to plug into the all-powerful God. As we explore the rhythm of the plug, we ask the following questions. What empowers you at the moment? How are you plugging into God? What gives you energy?

PLUGGING INTO A DIFFERENT POWER SOURCE

As we read through the Gospels we discover the wonderful example of Jesus rhythmically plugging into the loving care of the Father. In Luke 4:14 Jesus returned from the wilderness "with the power of the Spirit" (NRSV).

Jesus took measures to withdraw from everyday life, and the result was empowerment. Jesus needed power; so do we. Luke tells us that Jesus "would withdraw to deserted places and pray" (Luke 5:16 NRSV). In order to receive power Jesus pursued a lifestyle of regularly withdrawing and plugging in with prayer.

In Mark's Gospel these withdrawals show a very particular pattern:

In the morning, while it was still very dark, he got up and went out to a deserted place, and there he prayed. And Simon and his companions hunted for him. When they found him, they said to him, "Everyone is searching for you." He answered, "Let us go on to the neighboring towns, so that I may proclaim the message there also; for that is what I came out to do." And he went throughout Galilee, proclaiming the message in their synagogues and casting out demons. (Mark 1:35-39 NRSV)

In Mark's Gospel Jesus unplugs three times to specifically pray, and all three occurrences have to do with Jesus facing a crisis. In two of the instances crowds of people want to force him into a specific course of action.[1] In our community we jokingly say that a lot of people will tell you "God loves you" and subtly add "and I have a wonderful plan for your life." It was the same with the people in Jesus' life (Peter included)—they loved Jesus and they had specific ideas of God's plan for his life. But Jesus took time to calibrate his life with the Father's.

In the passage before Mark 1:35-39 Jesus experiences immense popularity. Mark tells us that the evening before the whole town gathered around the door, and Jesus healed many of the people (vv. 33-34). Early the following morning Jesus draws away from this popular hotspot in order to be in a desolate place. We can say that he unplugs from popularity in order to plug into God through prayer. Instead of feeding off the energy of the crowd, he finds an alternative energy source.

Meanwhile Peter (Mark still calls him Simon) and the other disciples searched for him; maybe they wanted to capitalize on this momentous popularity? I mean, this is the way to start a movement, right?

I often chuckle when I think of Jesus' PR strategy. In the book of Mark Jesus actively discourages the people touched by him from telling other people about him! Jesus goes against the power of the crowd and plugs into a different kind of narrative.

When Simon and the others search for him (Kenneth Wuest translates it as "they hunted him down"), Jesus decides to go to another town.[2] He can't be boxed in and is empowered to go in a different direction. Popularity is not the main ingredient of Jesus' narrative. Raw spirituality is not a popularity contest. Raw spirituality connects us to the unpredictable God.

In the second occurrence we read that Jesus multiplied the bread (Mark 6:30-44; John 6:1-15). The people view this amazing miracle and come to the conclusion that Jesus would be the perfect bread king; they want to make Jesus into their favorite image. Jesus is once again confronted with crowds ululating over him. John says, "When Jesus realized that they were about to come and take him by force to make him king, he withdrew again to the mountain by himself" (John 6:15 NRSV).

Faced with the prospect of becoming the king of the people, on their terms, Jesus unplugs and reengages in a different way. He reconnects with the Father when he is faced by the popularity of the crowd. We can learn some valuable insights from Jesus when we reflect on his withdrawals. It teaches us something about place, effects and reengagements.

Place. When Jesus unplugged and later plugged in, he chose a specific place. In Mark's Gospel it is called "a desolate place." The Greek word *erēmos* can also be translated as wilderness, wasteland and abandoned place.

It would be good for us to have a place or places to unplug as well. Without a specific place or space (which combines the concepts of geography and time) we will find it hard to unplug and then plug into the Author of life. About this space Henri Nouwen says,

> The very first thing we need to do is to set apart a time and a place to be with God and him alone. The concrete shape of this discipline of solitude will be different for each person depending

on individual character, ministerial task, and milieu. But a real
discipline never remains vague or general. It is as concrete and
specific as daily life. When I visited Mother Teresa of Calcutta
a few years ago and asked her how to live out my life as a priest,
she simply said: "Spend one hour a day in adoration of our Lord
and never do anything wrong, and you will be alright." She
might have said something else to a married person with young
children and something else again to someone living in a large
community. But like all great disciples of Jesus, Mother Teresa
affirmed again that ministry could only be fruitful if it grows out
of a direct and intimate encounter with our Lord.[3]

Nouwen reminds us that a time and a place (space) are important, and
that our arrangements cannot be vague or general. It is very important
to set up arrangements that are specific. The well-known acronym
SMART can help when we design our engagement with the rhythms
and particularly the invitation to plug in.

The **S** stands for *specific*; plugging in is not vague and general. The
M stands for *measurable*; it is concrete and specific and can be reflected on. The **A** stands for *achievable*; Mother Teresa didn't force
something on Nouwen that was impossible. The **R** stands for *relevant*;
Nouwen touches on the importance of our differing circumstances.
The **T** stands for *timely*—plugging in takes intention: like any relationship we need to schedule time together. These scheduled times lay
the foundation for later spontaneity.

SMART exercises help us to plug in to God because it takes our
differences into account. A plug-in rhythm for a mother of a four-
month-old will look different from that of a university student. It is
helpful to think through your specific life phase, your circumstances
and the unique personality you have. It is also important to remember
that plugging in is not something we add on to our lives. It is more
about integrating than addition.

Richard Foster uses a unique metaphor to explain this: "The spiritual life is not something we add onto an already busy life. What we are talking about is to impregnate and infiltrate and control what we already do with an attitude of service to God."[4] Plugging in is an invitation to impregnate our daily lives with God's empowering connections.

One of the well-known rhythms to plug in is Bible reading. I find that a lot of Christians are not fond of reading the Bible. (Many find it helpful to cure insomnia.) Yet, at some point during any given year, some people will be confronted with the "I need to read more Bible" intention. This voice usually echoes in the chambers of vagueness in a very non-SMART way and reverberates with unrealistic expectations.

I recently spoke to someone who is not reading the Bible at all. He told me that he wants to read through "the whole thing" in a month. As with dieting, this binge will only lead to discouragement.

Bashing through the Bible in a month is not smart. Together we explored what a SMART exercise could look like for his current reality. You might be surprised at the specific exercise that came out of our particular discernment conversation. My friend chose a very peculiar place and time to plug in. The toilet!

My friend downloaded the Bible on his smartphone and visited the bathroom armed with the SMART exercise of reading through a chapter in the New Testament during every sitting. His discipline did not suffer from vagueness or generality and was very concrete. His SMART exercise shows that we can plug in, in almost any place, which reminds me of a Teresa of Ávila story.

Teresa was praying through the liturgy while she ate a muffin. Nature called and she moved her devotions to the privy. As she sat in the outhouse, the devil confronted her about her irreverence in choosing this space. Teresa responded, "Devil, be gone! The prayers are for God. The muffin is for me and the rest is yours."[5]

I love this story because it shows that our *erēmos* can be any place. Raw spirituality develops plug-in rhythms in all of life; we learn how to practice the presence of God everywhere.

When my daughter, Tayla, was born, I used her midnight crying times to plug into God. During a very difficult week I got the dreaded It's-your-turn elbow from my wife. Sitting with Tayla in the rocking chair, I prayed the Jesus prayer over and over again, while I reflected on my anger at being awake.

I prayed, "Jesus Christ, Son of God, have mercy on me, a sinner." That week my SMART exercise was praying the Jesus prayer in the middle of the night when Tayla could not sleep. I remember praying that specific prayer almost three hundred times in the middle of one night. It was a space for transformation that helped me to deal with my anger and frustration.

When we lived in Colorado Springs I used a beautiful park called Ute Valley Park as my main *erēmos*. On a specific ledge I had the most amazing view of Pikes Peak. I had many plug-in sessions at this specific spot. When we relocated to Johannesburg, we flew out of Colorado on one of those crisp Colorado mornings with snow-capped Pikes Peak framing the background. We flew into the smog-filled atmosphere of Johannesburg, and I became extremely depressed at what I thought was the loss of my pristine *erēmos*.

A few weeks after we relocated I walked in Emmerentia, a local Johannesburg park, and murmured in the presence of God about the dirty streams and pollution in the city. I walked deeper into the park where it narrows and eventually runs perpendicular to one of Johannesburg's main roads named after Beyers Naudé, a minister who fought against the atrocities of apartheid. At its narrowest point I sat on a bench with a polluted stream in front of me. Behind me I heard the busy traffic. I asked God how I could withdraw in this place. This was not the kind of *erēmos* I envisioned. I opened the book of Proverbs and started reading in the first chapter:

Lady Wisdom goes out in the street and shouts.
   At the town center she makes her speech.
In the middle of the traffic she takes her stand.
   At the busiest corner she calls out:

"Simpletons! How long will you wallow in ignorance?
   Cynics! How long will you feed your cynicism?
Idiots! How long will you refuse to learn?
   About face! I can revise your life.
Look, I'm ready to pour out my spirit on you;
   I'm ready to tell you all I know.
As it is, I've called, but you've turned a deaf ear;
   I've reached out to you, but you've ignored me."
      (Proverbs 1:20-24)

These Scriptures reminded me of a childhood memory. When I
was a young boy, women from the neighboring farms would walk into
the city suburbs with bags of corn (called "mielies" in Afrikaans) on
their heads. They would shout loudly, "Mielies," and sell them to those
who heeded their call.

In the margin of my Bible I wrote down this childhood metaphor.
Maybe God was telling me that I could plug in, even in this place!
Maybe God can whisper wisdom in any kind of space. As I walked
out of the park I wrestled with the contrast between my Colorado
Springs *erēmos* and the stark filth of Johannesburg. As I reached my
car I almost dropped my keys when I heard the shout of a woman
with a bag of corn on her head, "Mielies!"

Your *erēmos* can be crafted wherever you are. It might be a park, a
room in your house, your car, a train or the bus ride you take every day.
It might be a sick bed, a vacation bed, a diaper changed or a honey-
moon bed. Maybe it is a beach or a mountain. It might be on a bike,
in a pool or jogging on a long road. It can be in the morning, afternoon or night. Or it might even be in congested traffic, a polluted

park or a squatter camp. In the life of Jesus we learn that any place can become an *erēmos*.

Effects. We are all plugged into networks that give us certain energies. These networks join us to stories or narratives. Social media through Twitter, Facebook and Instagram (to just name a few) provide us with story lines to live into. Some of these networks can be life giving. Others can be draining. In our plugged-in world we can now be more connected to someone on a different continent than our next-door neighbor.

When we plug in to God, we make a decision to unplug from other networks. Some of these networks deplete us: we unplug. Some of them energize us: we unplug. Regardless of their effects on us, we need to disconnect in order to plug in with God. This is called solitude.

In Mark 1:35-39 and John 6:1-15 we see how Jesus goes against the popularity network that wants to hang out with him as the Superman Jesus and reconnects with God's story of being the Suffering Servant. When Jesus withdraws, Peter (Simon) hunts him down and rebukes Jesus for his absence. It is as if Peter is saying to Jesus that there is great need and that everyone is looking for him. New Testament scholar James Edwards notes that the Greek word used for seeking—"Everyone is seeking you"—is used ten times in Mark and that it always carries a negative connotation. It describes a seeking that comes with impulses of manipulation and control.[6]

I am reminded that I sometimes seek out God in ways that are designed to control God. I co-opt God into my story. Plugging in can become attempts to get God to do what I want. This is toxic.

When Peter tries to convince Jesus with his PR strategy, Jesus firmly says no. Seeking God in the wilderness becomes a furnace where our impure motives and controlling tendencies burn away. When we plug in, we change.

In South Africa we have a huge challenge with electricity in the informal settlements (sometimes referred to as squatter camps). In these settlements some residents tap into the main power line without paying. Not only are these illegal connections made at great cost to the electricity companies, they are also extremely dangerous to those making the connections. Every year people are killed in their attempts to tap into these illegal energy sources. This is an apt metaphor for all the ways I access power in unhealthy and potentially deadly ways.

I have access to large quantities of counterfeit power. These are networks I need to unplug from.

This year during Lent I decided to unplug from Twitter and Facebook for forty days and use the time I would have spent on social media plugging in to God. It was hard. During the last few weeks of Lent I noticed that I get a lot of power through my social-network status checking and updating. I experienced some withdrawal symptoms from my experiment.

My addiction to social networks can become an illegitimate connection if it starts to dominate my life. It is the same with the Internet. I am typing this after a long weekend that was particularly hard for me. It was tough because the main Internet cable connecting the continent of Africa with Europe got severed. For four days Internet traffic in South Africa came to a screeching halt. It freaked me out. I was in a wilderness, of sorts.

Using the Mark passage as a dialogue partner I can say that I was hunted by my addiction for status checking and Internet connectivity. When I unplug the connections or networks I am usually plugged into, they hunt me.

Although unplugging can be hard, it is only the first half of the rhythm. We unplug not for the sake of unplugging but in order to plug in to a different power source. Saying no is followed by the beautiful invitation to the Person of *yes*.

If I only focus on the no, I will miss the relational invitation. I know all about missing the point. When I became a pastor, I served on a church staff that fasted every Thursday. We unplugged from the energy of food in order to connect with our energetic God. I battled with this because I only practiced the *no* part.

Every Thursday I would start my fast with great gusto. Then, during lunch, I would sit with people who were eating, murmuring how hard it was not to eat. My no to food didn't lead me to a yes to God. My fasting didn't connect me to feasting. When I decided to use the time I would spend eating to pray and connect with God, the unplugging led me to a new connection with God. We unplug to plug in.

In classic formation language plugging in is known as the disciplines of engagement, and unplugging is known as the disciplines of abstinence. I am writing this during the season of Lent. It is popular during Lent to give up something. Commonly, people ask, "What are you giving up for Lent?"

A few years ago I asked a trusted friend the same question, to which he responded, "I am adding twenty minutes of silence every day." At first I thought his answer was witty, but then I realized that it helps to focus on the plugging in instead of just the unplugging. In order for my friend to add twenty minutes of silence, he is saying no to something. But his answer keeps the focus in the right place. Many times our Lenten fasts and our disciplines can get stuck in the unplugging mode. We become bitter people saying no to everything and yes to no one.

How do I know when to unplug? Doesn't it sound legalistic and like a negation of God's beautiful gifts?

Whenever a desire that I have becomes disordered and is placed above God, it is time for some unplugging. Here is Paul on this subject: "Just because something is technically legal doesn't mean that it's spiritually appropriate. If I went around doing whatever I thought I could get by with, I'd be a slave to my whims" (1 Corinthians 6:12).

God gives us desires. These desires need to be ordered under God. Whenever desires become more important than God—or become sources of energy apart from God—they become "disordered desires."

Coffee is good. My desire for coffee is also good, unless it becomes a source of energy apart from God. I might for instance say, "For me to be creative I have to get a caffeine kick. I can't write without coffee." Now my coffee desire has become an ultimate source of power and has become disordered. My coffee drinking needs to be placed in the right order.

The language of plugging out and plugging in, with its movement toward withdrawal, gets used in the arena of addictions. When someone attempts to break an addiction, they go through "withdrawal symptoms." Living entangles us with all kinds of addictions.

As we unplug we will be hunted. This hunting might reveal some of our addictions. The hunting might come from people or withdrawal symptoms from our own bodies. Unplugging reveals our entanglement and allows us to reengage with God's story.

When my activities on Twitter or Facebook, watching television series, or coffee drinking become uncoordinated, disordered and excessive, it is time for some unplugging. Addiction to certain activities is a great possibility in our ad-saturated world.

However, it might be that my coffee drinking, Facebook checking and tweeting might be in line with and become a way of being plugged in with God—energizing others. However, I have to be mindful of the ways that I can rationalize this kind of thinking. Having a discerning friend is really helpful.

Dallas Willard notes that some of the most famous unplugging disciplines (abstinence) include solitude, silence, fasting, frugality, chastity, secrecy and sacrifice. The disciplines of plugging in (engagement) include study, worship, celebration, service, prayer, fellowship, confession and submission. These two lists are not the be all and end all of the discipline lists. You can also look at Richard Foster's excellent book *Celebration of Discipline*, John Ortberg's *The Life You've Always Wanted* or the spiritual exercises described in the Apprentice series by James Bryan Smith.

The Christian tradition has a vast treasury of plugging in and out disciplines that might stir your imagination. The key is to start small and to take your everyday life into account. Times change, and we need to creatively plug in—even on the toilet!

Reengagement. Plugging in is an invitation to connect with our beautiful God that synchronizes us toward a closer engagement with God's wild, adventurous kingdom. We connect with the King in order to become active participants in his kingdom. Plugging in changes us so that we can become a loving presence in the world. It connects us with our God revealed in the face of Jesus. In our yes to God we become a yes for the world. Plugging in does not merely provide us with energy to maintain the status quo.

One of the biggest challenges in our postmodern society is the ever-increasing speed we run at. The purpose of plugging in is not just to recharge our batteries and become more energized within the cultural status quo. Plugging in is not designed to energize us in the rat race. Plugging in provides the space where we can recalibrate our purposes toward those God envisions for the world and us.

Archbishop Desmond Tutu is a wonderful example of this. In 1976 he wrote a powerful letter to the prime minister of South Africa denouncing the inhumanity of apartheid. Before writing the letter Tutu plugged into God during a five-day retreat, and that encounter changed and repurposed him. When Tutu reflects on why he wrote the letter, he notes, "I felt this pressure, I had to do this and just sat at my desk. It more or less wrote itself."[7]

Tutu plugged in and wrote a courageous letter exposing the inhumanity of white Christians fueled by a toxic spirituality. His engagement with God moved him toward real issues in the world.

In the Mark passage we read that Jesus prayed, then he was hunted down and confronted with the agenda of his disciples and the crowd. When Peter voiced the plans they had for Jesus, Jesus responded, "Let us go on to the neighboring towns, so that I may proclaim the message there also; for that is what I came out to do" (Mark 1:38 NRSV).

Jesus moves into the wilderness and prays. Out of this engagement he reconnects with God's purpose: "that is what I came out to do." Edwards notes that there is a suggestive parallel in the phrase *came out* in the Markan passage. First Jesus "went out" to the wilderness, and then he explains that he "came out" in order to proclaim the message. Jesus moves in the graceful two-step of an inward and outward rhythm. His intimate connection with the Father compels him to lovingly engage the world.[8]

Spirituality for the sake of the world honors this dynamic inward and outward movement. Unfortunately we can easily miss this creative tension and get stuck on the inward or the outward movements. If we get stuck on the outward mode, we can easily burn out or suffer from "compassion fatigue."[9]

In my experience, people with privilege usually get stuck in the inward phase. The word *retreat* epitomizes this stuckness. For some people a retreat offers them the time to get away and recharge their batteries in order to run the rat race with new vigor. Retreats can be very unwilderness-like, and when churches organize retreat events, the setting usually smells of intense privilege.

I sometimes wonder what it would look like to send some of our brothers and sisters who suffer daily to a comfortable retreat center, and for our privileged brothers and sisters to go to wilderness spaces that smack more of wilderness?

What would it look like if we took pains to keep the creative tension between the inward and outward movements? We plug in so that we can be energized in our relationship with God, and through this plugging in we understand something of our belovedness. But this is not the be all and end all of plugging in. So many of our devotional practices stop at this place and become a stuck record that narcissistically repeats, "Jesus loves me."

A few years ago, as I read through the Gospel of Luke, I noticed something of the dynamic that took place in Jesus' relationship with the Father. A circular diagram can represent this dynamic. In the middle of the diagram a pictures of Jesus laughing.

In Luke's writings the energetic Jesus is continually engaged in a dynamic of experiencing his belovedness, being formed, receiving empowerment and being sent. This is illustrated in figure 3.2.

Figure 3.2. The inward and outward dynamic

When we plug in to God, it engages us somewhere in this dynamic, and sometimes all of these areas are synergized.

In Luke 3:22 we read how Jesus hears the wonderful words "you are my Son, the Beloved; with you I am well pleased" (NRSV). When we plug in we have the wonderful opportunity to reconnect with the voice that validates us with whispers of pleasure and desire. Plugging in makes room to listen and recalibrate our identity. We plug in to reaffirm our *belovedness*. Some of us desperately need to hear this voice, and retreating might help with this. God's initiating love starts the dynamic. God moves first toward us and then toward other people.

I find it highly suggestive that in Luke's Gospel the scene of Jesus experiencing his belovedness is followed by a genealogy, which I am always tempted to skip. I wonder if Luke is not purposefully slowing us down and reminding us that God's love permeates the cracks of all creation, specifically all those names that I want to skip.

Maybe Luke puts in the genealogy to remind us that people matter, to slow us down.

Raw spirituality delves into the genealogies and the specifics of people's lives and stories. Abstraction is perilous for our with-God lives.

When our daughter, Tayla, was two years old, she taught me a valuable lesson that I now refer to as the mathematics of love. She sat outside, baking in the African sun. In a circle around her she had gathered a handful of small rocks of different shapes and sizes, and she wanted to count them.

She took the first rock and said, "This is a daddy rock," then "This is a mommy rock" followed by "This is a brother rock" and "grandma rock" and "granddad rock," and then she continued with her mathematics of love. She used her familial genealogy to make sense of the rocks. She used a relational mathematics of naming. After watching my daughter perform this poetic act of counting, I could never look at a genealogy the same. People matter. God practices mathematics of love. We are loved and live among a long genealogy of others who are also loved.

Jesus' belovedness leads to his *formation* in the wilderness. We read that Jesus, "full of the Holy Spirit, returned from the Jordan and was led by the Spirit in the wilderness" (Luke 4:1 NRSV). Some people get stuck in the beloved phase and never move toward formation. We can fall into a narcissistic spirituality that is all about "me and Jesus" against "them out there." Being stuck on the beloved part of the dynamic can blind us to the rest of the people in our world.

Imagine Desmond Tutu on his five-day retreat worshiping and praying and thanking God for the fact that he is loved—but then doing nothing. Tutu recounts that during the retreat he felt a certain pressure.[10] Our belovedness pressurizes us into the flow of God's stream of love for all people. We are loved in order to love. Tutu describes the pressure:

> I don't quite know how to describe "God-pressure." There is a physical sensation, breathlessness, and a sense of being weighed down by a heavy burden. But neither of those is the main thing. The main thing is the sense of compulsion. It is a loving compulsion. But "God-pressure" is a feeling of being compelled to act, even against the voice of reason.[11]

Jesus feels God pressure. He returns from the experience with the Voice. The word *return* is a favorite word for Luke and shows the dynamic I am describing. Luke uses it thirty-two of the thirty-five times it is used in the New Testament. It is as if Luke is saying that we can't stay in one place. Raw spirituality is a spirituality of the road. The invitation is to move on; it is engagement on a journey. The danger is to get stuck.

It is instructional to see that Jesus' belovedness didn't lead to an infinite loop wherein he sang to the Father at successive conferences or church services. Jesus moves on. The love of God compels. As we are loved, we engage in a formational journey.

Jesus experiences his belovedness and moves into the wilderness. When Mark narrates that Jesus was led by the Spirit into the wilderness, he uses the Greek word *ekballō*, which is frequently used for driving out demons. "The Spirit immediately drove him out into the wilderness" (Mark 1:12 NRSV). This is a very specific God pressure!

It reminds me of the beautiful image of God as a maternal eagle shoving the baby eagles out of the nest.

> He found him out in the wilderness,
>   in an empty, windswept wasteland.
> He threw his arms around him, lavished attention on him,
>   guarding him as the apple of his eye.

He was like an eagle hovering over its nest,
   overshadowing its young,
Then spreading its wings, lifting them into the air,
   teaching them to fly. (Deuteronomy 32:10-11)

Some people are terribly frightened when they are sent into a wilderness; they think that they must have done something wrong. For them the purpose of plugging in is only to experience their belovedness and to shield them from the wilderness. But God forms us and teaches us to fly within his kingdom.

Now don't get me wrong, there are times when we need to camp at the beloved station or stay in the nest. Some people are so hurt and burned out that they need extensive times of encouraging love. Maybe you are so hurt right now that you find the thought of "God pressure" too daunting. Don't feel pressured, my friend—revel in your belovedness and allow God to graciously pressure you. When the time is right, God will woo you in the wilderness (Hosea 2:14).

Jesus is beloved and sent to be formed in the wilderness. Luke uses another *returned* statement to move the dynamic further: "Jesus returned to Galilee powerful in the Spirit. News that he was back spread through the countryside" (Luke 4:14). Being the beloved and experiencing "God pressure" toward formation leads to *empowerment*.

Do you remember Archbishop Tutu's comment that the letter almost wrote itself? He experienced a specific empowerment. Jesus the Beloved was formed in the wilderness and then empowered for the *missio Dei*. We read,

The Spirit of the Lord is on me,
   because he has anointed me
   to proclaim good news to the poor.
He has sent me to proclaim freedom for the prisoners

and recovery of sight for the blind,
    to set the oppressed free,
        to proclaim the year of the Lord's favor. (Luke 4:18-19 NIV)

Jesus experiences that he is loved. His identity of belovedness flows into a formational experience in the wilderness that leads to his empowerment. This power (remember my son Liam's story) gives him the ability to fulfill the mission he was *sent* to fulfill.

Luke tells us that Jesus started this mission in a very interesting place: "When he came to Nazareth, where he had been brought up, he went to the synagogue on the sabbath day, as was his custom. He stood up to read" (Luke 4:16 NRSV). Jesus is loved, formed, empowered and sent—to his hometown. There in the everyday of his hometown, Jesus engages the people as the beloved, formed, empowered and sent one. And it is tough.

When we plug in, we encounter the good and beautiful God who lovingly pressures us into a process of formation so that we can be empowered for our mission to specific people in our lives. It starts close and becomes a dynamic adventure of exploring a raw spirituality through which we plug in to God as loved, formed, empowered and sent people.

Training Naked

FOR REFLECTION AND DISCUSSION

1. Describe your ideal *eremōs*.

2. What is the reality of your current *eremōs*?

3. In what part of the dynamic are you currently finding yourself (beloved, formed, empowered, sent)?

4. Which God pressures have you felt in your life?

INDIVIDUAL EXERCISE

Design a SMART plug-in exercise and train with it. During the week remind yourself to plug in whenever you plug in a gadget.

GROUP EXERCISE

1. Share with the group which part of the dynamic you find yourself in.
2. Design a collective exercise for the next week. Go to rawspirituality.org and share the SMART exercises you designed.

FOUR

Irritating One Another

*The aim of God in history is the creation of an all-inclusive
community of loving persons with God himself at the
center of this community as its prime Sustainer
and most glorious Inhabitant.*

RENOVARÉ

*To belong to a community is to act as a creator and co-owner
of that community. What I consider mine I will build and nurture.
The work, then, is to seek in our communities a wider and
deeper sense of emotional ownership; it means fostering
among all of a community's citizens a sense
of ownership and accountability.*

PETER BLOCK

*Let us study how to irritate one another
to love and good works.*

HEBREWS 10:24 (PARAPHRASE)

I am writing this chapter during a very difficult time. A few weeks ago, in the third week of Lent, Lollie's parents were involved in a huge accident. Dad broke his hip and arm; his ribs also were fractured. During the days after the accident he experienced several complications due to the accident. Fat embolisms clogged his lungs, and he spent two weeks on a ventilator, sedated.

It was hard to live through this painful episode. Each day oscillated on the raw hinge of life and death. As Lent concluded in the celebration of Easter Sunday, Dad opened his eyes for the first time. With the celebration of Christ's resurrection he blew Mom a kiss and smiled. We were ecstatic.

Healing comes slowly. Daily we pilgrimaged to the intensive care unit. It was a tough time for us.

But.

We were overwhelmed by the love and support our family and friends gave us. Yesterday a friend invited me to a lunch at his house. He baked bread, brewed some coffee, and opened his heart and table to me. We all need bread-breaking, coffee-brewing friends.

It is impossible to walk the Jesus journey without close companions. I need friends that will sit in the valley of suffering with me. I am also invited to be that kind of friend for others.

A few weeks before the accident, my niece was born in the same hospital where Dad fought for healing. That was a day of joy, a vista created by the birth of a beautiful new life. It was an exuberant time. I need friends who will celebrate the joyful times with me. I am also invited to be that kind of friend for others. The rhythms of suffering and celebration mark the outer boundaries of the melody of authentic community. In between the boundaries of suffering and joy we live our everyday, ordinary lives together. This is the broad curriculum of a raw spirituality.

The apostle Paul alludes to this curriculum when he describes followers of Jesus as the body of Christ: "If one part hurts, every other part is involved in the hurt, and in the healing. If one part flourishes, every other part enters into the exuberance" (1 Corinthians 12:26). As followers of Jesus we learn the dialects of death and resurrection; community is the classroom where we become apt in the grammar of joy and suffering.

Fostering relationships takes time and intentionality. I cannot engage in friendships speedily. Loving God and others invites us into the beautiful rhythm of community. The bread-and-wine rhythm engages the question, Who are your companions that you journey with (see fig. 4.1)?

As we walk the on the Jesus journey, we need companions with whom we foster relationships around the everyday barbeque fires, kitchen tables, tailgate parties, coffee shops, restaurants and Eucharist celebrations of our lives.

Figure 4.1

Maybe you can stop now and reflect on the people you are currently journeying with. Start with your biological family. It is a sad reality that some people become so excited about spiritual formation that they sidestep their families. Family is a primary training site for godliness. Martin Luther noted that husbands and wives should have deep love for each other since they are each other's nearest neighbors.[1]

Next, reflect on the names of the people who are your 3 a.m. friends. These are the people you feel comfortable phoning in the early morning hours and vice versa.

One of my friends imagines the people she journeys with in concentric circles, with those closest to her forming an inner ring. She understands that we might have many acquaintances but only a few close companions. We have a limited capacity for close-knit friendships.

A few years ago I had a heart attack and underwent a triple bypass surgery. This incident revealed my 3 a.m. friends. In the aftermath of my recovery I spent another three days in an ICU more than four hundred miles from home. On the second day of my hospitalization my friend Carel walked into the room. It was an incredible act of companionship. He spent an hour with me and drove another four-hundred-plus miles home. We all need eight-hundred-mile friends—and to become those kinds of friends.

WHAT IS CHURCH?

Whenever we explore our travel companions and the contours of our journey, we enter the territory of describing church.

With the dawn of the new millennium Lollie and I resigned our positions at an influential megachurch in South Africa. We experienced an ecclesial (the fancy word for church) crisis. A few things fed into the crisis.

We were burned out. Long hours working at the church eroded the vitality of our faith. Church became synonymous with work, especially the programs. Church was not the people anymore. Church became abstract and people turned into numbers. The journey became impersonal. We reduced church to the weekend service; all our energies were spent on planning, designing and preaching a Sunday service. We were exhausted.

We were not rooted in Jesus (Colossians 2:6-8). Our roots were embedded in the strategies of church growth. This meant that the taproot of our existence was formed in the various leadership models coming from Harvard. We lost our connection to the Carpenter of Nazareth. We weren't living from the vine (John 15:1-11) but in Ivy League schools. Leadership models took the place of Jesus' example. In the name of relevance and practicality, Jesus was not our center. We didn't live as companions of Jesus.

We were church idolaters deeply addicted to the institution. The church became our all-encompassing reality. The church gave us purpose in life. The church provided us with a salary. The church was our life and, like all idols, it drained the life out of us. We wrongly believed that we had to grow the church. In our minds a big church meant success; a small church signified irrelevance. Success became our driving narrative. Church became our God. Edward Abbey noted that "growth for the sake of growth is the ideology of the cancer cell."[2] We had church cancer, and it was malignant.

So in 2000 we resigned with a huge question aching in our hearts: What is church? From 2000 to 2003 we lived with this question in the United States. In those days it became popular to talk about the ABCs of church. Everywhere young twentysomethings were deconstructing church as "**A**ttendance, **B**uildings and **C**ash." This was the era of the blossoming of the blogosphere and emergent gatherings. Coffee shops became Parisian posses and the spirit of Derrida was active and alive. Deconstruction was the grammar of choice.

We became experts in asking the What is church? question and developed fantastic critiques deconstructing church. One particular day I made a list in the back of Eugene Peterson's book *Under the Unpredictable Plant.*[3] The column's heading read "Church is not." My list was extensive. Articulating what church *is not* came easy. It was my spiritual gift to populate this list.

I started another column with the heading "Church is." It was harder to complete this list. When deconstruction becomes a primary language, it can be dangerous and lead to bitterness. I know what it means to live a constant negative; it drains energy and saps creativity.

Peterson's book *Under the Unpredictable Plant* explores the life of Jonah as a narrative for pastoral faithfulness. Peterson contrasts vocation with careerism. Like Jonah we are called to go to a specific Nineveh, but then we escape to Tarshish, his metaphor for a career.

I knew what it meant to be a professional Christian working for a church. What would it mean to follow my vocation toward the person of Jesus?

With our green cards eight months away we heard the call from

God to go back to South Africa. Johannesburg was our Nineveh. Here, we discovered companions for the next leg of our journey.

JESUS FIRST

Back in Johannesburg we gathered with a group of friends who were also asking, What is church? We soon found out that this is not a fruitful primary question. This question tends to turn us inward. It can mislead us. Because Jesus owns the church, it is paramount that we don't make an idol of it. We realized that a better question to ask is, Who is Jesus? The church is not the hope of the world—Jesus is (Colossians 1:27; 1 Timothy 1:1 ; 1 Peter 1:3-4). This is not just semantics.

When Paul explores the church he emphasizes the centrality of Jesus:

> And when it comes to the church, he organizes and holds it together, like a head does a body.
>
> He was supreme in the beginning and—leading the resurrection parade—he is supreme in the end. From beginning to end he's there, towering far above everything, everyone. So spacious is he, so roomy, that everything of God finds its proper place in him without crowding. (Colossians 1:18-19)

Alan Hirsch follows this Pauline injunction and articulates the need to develop our churches from the centrality of Jesus. Our Christology will lead to our missiology, which will lead to our ecclesiology. The sequence is important.[4] Jesus first, then mission and then church.

When we move the church question to the front we enter the murky waters of idolatry. It is surprising to me that Jesus didn't talk about church all that much. In one of his most pronounced statements on the church he reminds us that he will build his church (Matthew 16:13-20). That is why I feel uncomfortable calling myself a "church planter." I feel more like a person responding to Jesus building his church than someone initiating or planting.

We can't build the church with any great idea, plan or management.

The church is built by Someone else. As we follow Jesus, our collective rhythms of love, life and obedience become the church. Jesus makes it happen. Church is the accidental byproduct of people relating to Jesus' life, death and resurrection. As we crash into Jesus, a kingdom explosion takes place.

Placing Jesus first and not drowning in the church question is really hard. When we reduce the church to a building and engineer it through various programs, we fall into the trap of building an idol.

One evening Lollie and I listened to a testimony evening in which members of a prominent worldwide church movement testified to their changed lives. Testimony after testimony rung with the following two phrases: "then the church changed my life" and "the pastors of this church changed my life." In more than ten testimonies Jesus wasn't mentioned once. A church without Jesus becomes an idol. This idolatry is something I know from the inside. Inside my veins runs the poison of this ideology.

When we are trapped in the church question without focusing on Jesus, discipleship suffers. Exploring church without Jesus is an unfortunate possibility and leads us astray. Henri Nouwen wisely states,

> If you were to ask me point blank: "what does it mean to live spiritually?" I would have to reply "Living with Jesus at the center." There are always countless questions, problems, discussions, and difficulties that demand one's attention. Despite this, when I look back over the last thirty years of my life, I can say that, for me, the person of Jesus has come to be more and more important. Specifically, this means that what matters increasingly is getting to know Jesus and living in solidarity with him. There was a time when I got so immersed in problems of church and society that my whole life had become a sort of drawn-out, wearisome discussion. Jesus had been pushed into the background or had himself become just another problem. Fortu-

nately, it hasn't stayed that way. Jesus has stepped out front again, so to speak, and asked me: "And you, who do you say that I am?" It has become clearer to me than ever that my personal relationship with Jesus is the heart of my existence.[5]

I remember the first time when I read these words. It cut me deep. I reflected on my day-to-day conversations and evaluated how many chats centered on church and how many on the person of Jesus. If I counted the ratio between church and Jesus conversations in a given day, the scoreboard often read: Church 23, Jesus 2.

The journey with the person of Jesus (also called the Way) was reduced to a constant focus on the container: the church. This had to change.

DETOXING: AKA THE HABIT OF ADVENTURE

In 1948 the Quaker author Elton Trueblood wrote a small book called *An Alternative to Futility* (catchy title, isn't it?). In it he describes the American church after World War II and how people experienced their lives as futile. Even the church became a place of unimaginative life. Trueblood gives the following description of the lifeless church.

> The basic defect of the Protestant churches lies not in their divided condition but in their insipidity. They show so little imagination. The same kind of dull and lifeless service is repeated endlessly, whatever the occasion. We are in a time of crisis when we need a dynamic fellowship to turn the world upside down. What we are offered is a stereotype. A man, having become convinced that we are in a race with a catastrophe, may seek the very bread of life, but in practice he is forced to sing sentimental songs with words he does not mean, listen to some comforting platitudes, and finally shake the minister's hand at the door, because there is no other way to escape![6]

Trueblood advocates for a church willing to experiment and to engage culture with imagination, dreaming, modest experiments, boldness, courage and radical, real membership. Above all else, "it is at least clear that the society must make the habit of adventure central to its life."[7]

When we gathered as a new church plant, we needed a serious detox from the poisons of church as ideology. We attempted to build the habit of adventure. This meant that we had to face some of our own unimaginative and insipid ways. We described our habit of adventure as a detox. The following is a list of our initial antioxidants:

- follow Jesus and not the pastor
- seek the kingdom of God above all else
- exercise daily disciplines to become more like Jesus
- as a family member share my life with others
- get to know the text and live into it
- realize that I am a missionary and have a full-time calling
- respect the wider church over geography and time
- confess our brokenness and journey toward wholeness
- give sacrificially, especially money and time
- reach out to the poor

These antioxidants were invitations to turn our attention away from church ideology to following Jesus and his kingdom invitations. We were attempting to move beyond deconstruction and getting the poison out of our systems through modest experiments. Together we were slowly becoming the people of the Way.

To live into these antioxidants we attempted to align our embodied community rhythms with the life of Jesus. I want to emphasize this. We weren't just doing the same things and calling it a different name. I sometimes think this is at the heart of a lot of church change.

Churches do the same things and just name them differently. They were *seeker*, then *emerging*, then *missional*—but during these different transitions they were doing exactly the same thing. Change won't happen when we engage in linguistic gymnastics.

We were experimenting to go beyond church ABCs—attendance, buildings and cash. We were retraining our lives and bodies toward the *D* of the ABCDs—*discipleship*.[8] We ventured to connect afresh with Jesus by reskilling our stunted imaginations.

Let me unpack some of these antioxidants a bit further. This detox program was very context specific, so please don't read this as pre-scriptive—every community has to work out their own detox program.

First, placing Jesus in the center cannot happen without engaging with the writings of Matthew, Mark, Luke and John. In these texts the Holy Spirit depicts God through the stories of Jesus. We pored over these texts and immersed ourselves in the Gospel.

Most of us were used to "copy and paste" versions of Bible reading: we lifted some passages out of context and pasted them under a point we wanted to make. Our lives were the dominant script, and we searched for a text to rationalize our story.

Our detox meant that we read each Gospel in its original context as God's Story, which invited us to become part of a new adventure within our unique circumstances. The Author of the story pulled us into a whole new way of being humans.

Second, before every sermon, the community divided into small groups, read the text and discussed it for at least ten minutes.

It was tough.

We found that many church members have voluminous years of pent up teachings inside of them, and when we give them the chance, they will unleash it on their group. It is easier to dump info on a group than explore personal reflections. We found that some people suffered serious verbal diarrhea. Listening to each other became a huge chal-lenge. These groups became mini training grounds where we learned the skills of listening, honoring and respecting each other.

Some people tolerated the group times; they wanted to hear "what the real answer was." Many people didn't trust that God could speak to them through other "untrained" people, or that God might be working through them.

After the small groups discussed the passage, we got some feedback in the large gathering. People shared what happened in their groups. Some shared, while others voiced questions. I stood amazed at what came out of the groups. I would spend more than ten hours in preparation with the text and miss some of the amazing insights people discovered there. These conversations became invitations for conversion. Our meetings became sites of learning and unlearning. We broke the monopoly of the professional person with the microphone. It wasn't romantic; growth seldom is.

After our first experiment with this kind of dialogue we debriefed in the evening. People wanted to know whether our discussions were really allowed in a church service. "Was it legitimate church?" Church ideology was deeply embedded in our imaginations.

Third, as a part of our detox we started to follow the liturgical calendar used by the worldwide church. Every week we read together with the universal church (usually the Revised Common Lectionary) and became part of the church year's liturgical rhythms of Advent, Epiphany, Lent, Pentecost and Ordinary time. Slowly but surely we discovered what it meant to follow Jesus on a different timetable and to become part of a bigger story.

Fourth, we were detoxing from understanding church as a noun and living into what church could mean as an adventurous verb. To help us we didn't own a church building. We don't think it is wrong to own a building. We just know how hard it is to not think of church as the building. Language became important to us.

If we were going to imagine something different, we had to relearn how we speak. One of the comments we attacked head-on is "On

Sunday I am going to church." Whenever I or anyone else used this phrase, we would ask what was meant by it. Is it a reference to the Sunday service and the community hall we rented? In many Sunday schools we teach the children that church is not the building but the people. Then we contradict this with everything we do and say after that particular class. Followers of Jesus are the church; the church includes the Sunday service but is so much more.

Fifth, because we are members of each other, we would miss those who couldn't gather on a Sunday. It became popular for people to let the rest of the members know where they were. For instance, "the church of Jacques and Anne-Marie will be helping someone to move this Sunday" or "the church of Sakkie and Lindie will be on holiday and won't be at the gathering."

Now for a word of confession and transparency. As a pastor I want people to come to the gathering to hear my sermon. This can become an ego thing. It was for me. When people catch the vision that church is about more than a one-man or one-woman sermon and singing a few hymns, the pastor will possibly experience some issues of ego deflation. I felt it. Moving people's narrative from church as Sunday at a building listening to my sermon to church as people playing in the kingdom of God brings freedom to some and loss to others. I think this loss might be one of the reasons why we don't see churches changing—it is hard for many pastors to move from center stage.

Sixth, detoxing from consumerism became important. At least once a month we would engage with the following liturgy in our meetings.

Leader: This is called a church service.
          Why is it called a church service?
          Is it because you are paying a pastor to render you a service?

People: No.
          We are all gathered to render a service to God.

Full engagement with the liturgy meant that we democratized the microphone and deconstructed church as a show or performance. I, as the pastor, could not run the show. Community cannot grow through the voice of one person. The service we render to God is the responsibility of all, not just the worship band and the preacher (1 Corinthians 14:26).

The word *liturgy* literally means "the work of the people." We were attempting to get people to work. So I quit running the church. I quit administering the sacraments. (Our community is nondenominational, but I recognize that this approach won't fit every tradition.)

I will never forget our community's first celebration of the Eucharist after I "resigned." The person who volunteered to facilitate the Lord's Supper stood up and told the congregation that he almost phoned me the previous evening to cancel. He didn't believe that he was worthy to serve communion.

"You see," he said, "I am trapped in a vicious cycle of an addiction that overshadows my life."

He then explained to the congregation how he reckoned that he was too much of a sinner to administer this precious gift of the Lord's Supper. He looked down when he made this confession. Then, with tear-filled eyes, he looked up and said, "But then I realized that this is the purpose of this Table. It is a Table of grace. And if people like me are not welcome at this Table, then no one is."

In that broken, beautiful moment our community cracked open—"we carry this precious Message around in the unadorned clay pots of our ordinary lives" (2 Corinthians 4:7). We were slowly detoxing from church services designed to be productions that tend toward performances of perfection. The cracks allowed God to break through. The church is not a theater where some people perform and the rest become spectators or critics. Church is not the place where we perform. If that becomes our model of church, then an inordinate amount of time and energy will go into the Sunday service production. This leads to what I call, tongue in cheek, the "sexy worship leader syndrome."

I started using this term when a friend who became seriously disillusioned with church told me that her last day at a specific church's service was when she went through an extremely tough time. The script of her life represented intense chaos. However, the script of the church was perfect. Beautifully shaped people were singing perfectly rehearsed songs. The pastor eloquently delivered a finely crafted sermon. Everyone looked so sorted out. It was excellent, but it gave her no place to crack.

Instead of a clay pot, she encountered a crystal vase. I am not saying that church is a place where we don't strive toward excellence and doing things with a spirit of creativity. But I think excellence can easily slip into forms of consumerism.

Seventh, we realized that we were working with membership assumptions formed by health clubs, golf clubs and other consumer groups. A friend of mine who worked at a gymnasium in Johannesburg told me that they have a cupboard with over six hundred membership cards of people who signed up for the gym and never collected their cards! Unfortunately, many church members view belonging to the church in the same way. We wondered what it would look like to have church membership informed by Jesus and the church's traditions, and not the consumer models of other institutions.

So we took our antioxidant list and invited our community members to work out SMART exercises based on the list of our initial antioxidants. It worked this way: In January our church had no members. During this month prospective members would discern whether Claypot was the community through which they should serve Christ in the following year.

If prospective members discerned that Claypot was the people they would journey with, then they would take each antioxidant and work out a training plan for the year. At the end of January we would take a clay pot and break it on a Sunday. During the week we would come together to mend the pot. Here is a blog post I wrote after one of our ceremonies.

> Sunday we broke a clay pot and gave everyone a piece to write a prayer in. Last night was operation "put it all back together." Our evening was spent praying and playing. When we broke the pot, we placed it in a bag and threw it on the floor. The pot scattered into a lot of pieces. The community asked me, "Why didn't you use a hammer?"
>
> Putting the pot together taught us a lot. A few of our members couldn't be there last night and it reminded us how crucial each person's contribution is. Without their pieces we couldn't complete the mending process. Building a community takes patience and is not a quick result-oriented exercise.... A few pieces didn't fit with ease. We had to file and soften some of the edges produced by the scattering. After a lot of fine and delicate work the pieces fitted! A community is an opportunity for people to recalibrate ingrained individualistic tendencies to rhyme with others in a new harmony. This harmonizing is not a smooth process. When I asked Lollie's parents for her hand in marriage, her dad told me that a marriage is like two stones in a river. The stones constantly bump and chafe each other till the edges become smooth—ditto with a community. Glue is essential in repairing a broken pot. The adhesive must be strong and have the right thickness. Last night we used super- and putty glue. In one of the prayer times one of our members thanked Christ for being the glue in our community. Without Him we will not fit together. Our evening ended and we did everything we could do without all the pieces. The result was a shabby looking pot. Nothing spectacular or praiseworthy, a perfect picture of a congregation! Sinners journeying with God as the guide.[9]

All new members buddy up with an encourager who writes their friend's name in a journal. These friends or accountability partners (we now call them "encouragers") regularly meet and help each other with the detox and the SMART exercises.

Members who discerned that Claypot was not the people God called them to were commissioned and sent away during a special sending service. This was hard. Leaving is difficult, but the kingdom is bigger than our local churches.

Even with these antioxidants working its healing in our community, during 2006 we realized that the list was still too abstract. During that year the elders converted the list into the rule of life with the symbols making up chapters three to nine of this book. Let me tell you more about this process.

REGULA TO INVITATION

In September 2006 the elders went on a special weekend journey. In preparation for the weekend we read through the Gospels and looked at the concept of membership in the early church.

The discussion was deeply influenced by an article titled "Early Church Catechesis and New Christians' Classes in Contemporary Evangelicalism" by New Testament scholar Clinton E. Arnold.[10] Arnold contrasts the typical eight-week membership class of the contemporary church with the intense three-to-five-year membership journey during the first three centuries of the church.

Armed with a gospel-growing imagination and historical examples, we morphed the antioxidant list into a rule of life. Jim Smith notes that "Early Christian communities used the word *rule* to describe their strategy for growth. The idea of a rule comes from the Latin word *regula*, which refers to a rule or covenant that states your intentions."[11]

We developed seven pictures that we printed in a linear form underneath each other. Each picture represented a symbol and had a

Scripture reference with it. During the elder weekend we also typed a minimum requirement next to each picture. Next to the plug symbol we had "spend at least 15 minutes a day plugging in with God."

After a heavy debate we decided not to include the minimum standard under each symbol. As elders we invited congregants to engage with every picture or *regula* and work out the ways they could live it out in their daily lives. The elders shared the *regula* with the congregation and friends started training with it.

It was an immense learning time for us.

Every week people shared the imaginative ways they engaged with the different parts of the rule of life. We were moving away from a one-size-fits all spirituality toward a raw spirituality encompassing the varied rhythms of our unique lives.

During this time the language of *musts* crept into our vocabulary. Our friends Harold and Debbie made us aware how the beautiful invitations of Jesus were in danger of becoming lifeless lists. Spiritual formation can easily become technique. Without the relational invitation of Jesus encouraging us to engage with each of the symbols, they would become a new form of legalism. Raw spirituality cannot be engineered.

Tina and Gerrit Kruger, a gifted couple in our congregation, wrote a beautiful short drama in which they portrayed each symbol as an invitation to a party hosted by God. It helped us to bust the myth of obligation and to reorient ourselves toward the beautiful God who invites us into relationship. A few months into 2007 we started talking about the "invitations" instead of the *regula* or "rule of life," and now we refer to it as the "rhythms of life."

Our individualistic society tends to leave us with huge identity crises. Many people live in a constant dismembered state. Some people don't belong anywhere. With the advent of international travel we are experiencing an unprecedented dismembering of geography and of our families. Here in South Africa I frequently encounter the pain of families dealing with family and friends emigrating to other countries.

As communities we are challenged to move from dismembering to re-membering, or what Wendell Berry calls "connecting responsibly."[12] We are called to invite people to become part of something other than rugged individualism. It is an invitation to re-member (to) the family of God and become part of a new social structure modeled after our trinitarian God. The bread-and-wine symbol can also be called the "re-member rhythm."

Family is the choice word for the church gathered and sent. People on the journey are family. When we become part of a church we become part of a new big family with many brothers and sisters. "Brother" and "sister" aren't just handy titles when you forget someone's name in your church. Along with the designation of "brother" and "sister" come certain gifts and responsibilities.

Because we live in a constantly abstracting culture that reduces personal names and stories into numbers and statistics, we have to recover relational rhythms and root out words that depersonalize.

CONTOURS OF THE RE-MEMBER JOURNEY

Many people who have moved from understanding church as a place to a people are excited to leave the old thinking behind. They become zealous and often hurt those who don't get it. Well-intentioned and concerned friends will then warn them with variations of Hebrews 10:25: "not neglecting to meet together, as is the habit of some, but encouraging one another, and all the more as you see the Day approaching" (NRSV).

A conversation referencing this verse will usually come back to "don't develop a habit of not coming to the gathering(s)." As they use this verse, "the gathering" refers to the Sunday worship service. This proof text is then used to bring the new zealot back into the worship service.

However, consider that specific passage within its bigger context:

Let us hold fast to the confession of our hope without wavering, for he who has promised is faithful. And let us consider how to provoke one another to love and good deeds, not neglecting to meet together, as is the habit of some, but encouraging one another, and all the more as you see the Day approaching. (Hebrews 10:23-25 NRSV)

Notably the size of the gathering is not stipulated. It could be two or a half-million. And when we look at the verses preceding verse 25, the purpose of the gathering becomes clear: it is much wider than merely assembling together. The gathering should be characterized by stimulation toward love and good deeds. This purpose is attained through considering and encouraging one another.

Community can then be defined (using v. 24) as the place where we're considering how to stimulate one another to love and good deeds. In other words we "consider one another unto an outburst of love and good works."[13]

Here is where things get interesting.

Considering is mentioned more than once in the Hebrews letter. In Hebrews 3:1 we are encouraged to "consider Jesus." Now in Hebrews 10:24 we are invited to consider "one another."

The re-membering journey we are on keeps our eyes on Jesus and on one another. We pay attention to Jesus and our friends. This might be a good time to take out the list of friends you reflected on in the beginning of this chapter. In the Amplified Bible, Hebrews 10:24 is magnified in the following way: "And let us consider *and* give attentive, continuous care to watching over one another, studying how we may stir up (stimulate and incite) to love *and* helpful deeds *and* noble activities."

Studying is used here as a synonym for considering. When I look over my list, I am wondering how I can study my friends to stir them on to love and good works. I am also wondering how I am allowing my friends to do the same for me.

The word *stimulate* in Greek is *paroxysmon*, the source of the English word *paroxysm*. Descriptions associated with *paroxysm* are "fit, attack or seizure." Using this word we can then say that community is a group (as small as two) in which we study one another so that fits of love and good deeds can take place.

This particular word is used only twice in the New Testament. The other time is in Acts 15:36-41, where the paroxysm between Paul and Barnabas over Mark became so violent that they parted ways.

Some translations use the word *provoke*. Over the last few years our community has opted for the word *irritate* as a synonym for *provoke*.[14] It strikes us as dissonant that we should consider how we could irritate/provoke one another to love and good deeds. Irritation or provocation offers a healthy corrective to creating bread-and-wine communities where we engage in friendships with people who are just like us.

We all stand in danger of building a dream community with people who are just like us. The reason is that we don't like being irritated. So we build small enclaves and personal relationships with people of the same race, education, socioeconomic standing and faith. Somehow we believe that it is in our best interest to create this "wish dream."[15]

In the absence of irritation we find it easy to hang out with people living the same comfortable narrative, because they never study us or irritate us to love and good deeds.

The contours of the bread-and-wine journey span the ups and the downs of joy and suffering and everything in between. It takes place as we *consider* Jesus and each other. Love and good works are the outcome of this fellowship. As a community we study each other by asking good questions and encouraging each other to engage with Jesus and others for the sake of the world. Let's irritate each other to love and good deeds!

Training Naked

FOR REFLECTION AND DISCUSSION

1. Who are your companions on the journey (who sits at the table of your life, are your 3 a.m. friends, your inner circle)?

2. Take some time to reflect on the re-membering journey you are on with the friends on the list of question 1. What do you notice?

3. Reflect on an incident where a friend irritated you toward love and good deeds. How did you receive the irritation?

4. How can you study your friends in order to encourage them toward love and good deeds?

INDIVIDUAL EXERCISE

Go over the companion list you reflected on in this chapter. It might be helpful to have a conversation with the people you have listed. Do they know that you value them? Do they value you? In what way are you forming one another? Take some time this week to schedule individual time with your companions and talk about your thoughts.

GROUP EXERCISE

Gather as companions and discuss the following questions:

1. Which sufferings and joys are we bringing?

2. How can we detox from unhelpful community practices?

3. How are we studying one another?

4. How are we irritating one another?

Print out all the "one another" passages in Scripture and discuss how they pertain to your groups of companions.[16] What invitations do you see in those passages?

FIVE

Puzzling the City

‑‑‑

Be generous with the different things God gave you,
passing them around so all get in on it.

1 PETER 4:10

Let's just go ahead and be what we were made to be,
without enviously or pridefully comparing ourselves with
each other, or trying to be something we aren't.

ROMANS 12:5

As we plug in with our beautiful God and journey together, we
become a gang for goodness. In most gangster movies great detail
goes into explaining the different roles of the gang members. Almost
every gang has a getaway driver, a thief and an expert in disabling
alarms. In the kingdom gang for goodness we also have unique con-
tributions to make.

All of us have the sacred privilege of playing a role. God's plan can
be imagined as a puzzle. Each one of us represents a unique part of
the puzzle. As our puzzle pieces interlock, a beautiful picture emerges.
Together we make a collective contribution. However, when I remove

my unique contribution from the puzzle, we all suffer. Nothing spoils a puzzle like missing pieces.

In figure 5.1 the puzzle symbol reminds us that on our own we are not the whole puzzle. We partake in the grand tapestry of God's bigger Story. With the puzzle symbol we ask the question, *How am I a gift to the world through my unique contribution?*

Figure 5.1

THE STORY WE LIVE IN

Our uniqueness was born in the heart of God. We are fearfully and wonderfully made (Psalm 139:14 NRSV), and God wills for our unique lives to make a difference in the created world. In his Story we become actresses and actors. God uses our personality, gifts, passions, hobbies, temperaments, experiences and talents, and mixes all of it into a beautiful life-giving puzzle piece. As our pieces intermingle, shalom comes to the world. God uses gangs of goodness to make the world a better place.

Don Miller opens his book *A Million Miles in a Thousand Years* with a striking note. He imagines watching a movie about a person whose main ambition in life is to drive a Volvo. He notes that a movie about a guy who wants to buy a car won't excite us: "Nobody cries at the end of a movie about a guy who wants a Volvo. But we spend years actually living those stories, and expect our lives to feel meaningful."[1]

All of us live in a particular story. Stories are like big puzzles in which we figure where our piece fits. Don's point is not that God's people can't drive Volvos. But if *the* purpose of someone's life is driving a Volvo, then it is pointless. God can use our lives if we are willing to engage in the bigger Story we find ourselves in. But what is this story? A loving God makes the world a better place.

Father, Son and Spirit work toward a beautiful world. God loves the world (John 3:16) and activates artists to make it a better place:

"Inside you there's an artist you didn't know about."[2] We are invited to become part of the trinitarian beautifying life. I am invited to be one of these artists, and so are you! This beautifying takes place in the all-encompassing reality of grace. Here is how Paul describes it,

> Saving is all his idea, and all his work. All we do is trust him enough to let him do it. It's God's gift from start to finish! We don't play the major role. If we did, we'd probably go around bragging that we'd done the whole thing! No, we neither make nor save ourselves. God does both the making and saving. He creates each of us by Christ Jesus to join him in the work he does, the good work he has gotten ready for us to do, work we had better be doing. (Ephesians 2:8-10)

Grace saves and grace involves us in the work. Jesus died for us and rose so that we can live a new life. The Ephesians passage in the English Standard Version notes that we are God's "workmanship." *Workmanship* is a beautiful word in Greek, *poiēma*—we are God's poems. We join the poetry making of God. Our unique contribution becomes the art of the Artists.

Metanarrative is a fancy word describing the big story we find ourselves in. Imagine building a thousand-piece puzzle without the picture on the puzzle's box guiding you. Metanarratives are like the picture on the puzzle box. If you figure out what the picture is, then you can fit together the puzzle pieces. We live in different societies where many people battle to find the picture on the box. Some find a picture, but it destroys them. There are three destructive puzzle pictures: money, sex and power.

Jesus' followers follow Jesus. Jesus is the picture on our box. In the life, death and resurrection of Jesus we find a metanarrative worth following. Jesus' life reverberates into eternity. As I grew up my dad would often tell us that we all have to bring something to the party. In Jesus' life we understand the shape of the party.

Jesus partied a beautiful life. "I came feasting and they called me a lush, a friend of the riffraff. Opinion polls don't count for much, do they? The proof of the pudding is in the eating" (Matthew 11:19). We are invited to the Jesus party. In partying and puzzling we play our part.

I still remember my daughter Tayla's excitement when she participated in her first school play. She practiced her part incessantly. She knew what part of the puzzle she was and what that meant. Every waking moment became a rehearsal. She reenacted the drama before the drama. During the months before the concert Tayla had a very clear purpose. During the concert Tayla's practice and rehearsal allowed her to joyfully enter the experience. It brought all of us great joy.

This is a wonderful picture of what we are invited to when we follow Jesus. We are invited to rehearse the life we are going to live for an eternity, starting now. That is why we pray, "May your kingdom come, on earth as in heaven." We rehearse eternity by using our puzzle piece in our everyday ordinary lives.

As we get the picture on the puzzle box right, we participate. This participation is a joyful celebration. God loves our participation. It gives God great pleasure when we puzzle faithfully.

However, if the picture on our box is wrong—everything else collapses. When Paul and Peter write about being a part of the puzzle they both explore how followers of Jesus will have to disassociate from wrong pictures.

In 1 Peter 4, before we read that we have to serve with our puzzle piece (v. 11) we read:

> You've already put in your time in that God-ignorant way of life, partying night after night, a drunken and profligate life. Now it's time to be done with it for good. Of course, your old friends don't understand why you don't join in with the old gang anymore. But you don't have to give an account to them. (1 Peter 4:3-5)

When we join a gang for goodness, we connect with a new narrative. The picture on our puzzle box changes; our story undergoes a conversion. We enact a different kind of drama. Peter reminds his readers that their puzzle picture was one of partying—the hedonistic life. Now they live with a different picture. Peter prepares his listeners and tells them that their old gang will not be pleased by their new picture. In Jesus we become a new kind of human. We have the wonderful privilege of influencing our old gang with the love and goodness of the new story we live.

The apostle Paul also comes to this conclusion. Before he commands the Roman community to use the gifts given to them (Romans 12:6), he reminds them that they are to offer their bodies as a living sacrifice (v. 1). Furthermore, they should not pattern themselves in conformity to the world (v. 2). All of us are a puzzle piece in a particular puzzle. Our gang has a picture on the box. There are no one-man gangs.

I sometimes find myself in a story and a gang that I don't want to be in. Repentance is the process of patterning our lives to a different picture on the box and joining a different gang. The Jesus puzzle picture shows two great rhythms, love of God and love of others. When I discover the picture on the box, I enact a life of love. Like Tayla I rehearse that love in the here-and-now nitty-gritty details of my everyday life.

FANNING THE FLAME

I have done a fair share of tests to discover my puzzle piece. Some of these tests are amazing and helpful. Some of them are a bit dorky and can be deeply influenced by the kind of breakfast you ate. Just think of all the tests you have done in order to discover yourself. I can think of StrengthsFinder, DISC, Myers-Briggs and all those spiritual gift inventories. Maybe you are a bit like me. If I don't purposefully revisit these tests, I forget the results.

Sometimes I feel ashamed by my glib engagement with these results. It is a privilege to have this kind of access. I was reminded of this when my wife taught temperaments to underprivileged students. They soaked the results deep into their bones. It fired them up into the adventure of making a unique contribution.

Paul's admonition to Timothy comes to mind: "And the special gift of ministry you received when I laid hands on you and prayed—keep that ablaze! God doesn't want us to be shy with his gifts, but bold and loving and sensible" (2 Timothy 1:6-7).

My giftedness gives me clues about my unique puzzle piece. It helps me understand my story in the bigger Story. It fires me up and energizes those around me. Paul reminds Timothy to keep his unique gift ablaze. The reason for this is that we can let the flame of our gift languish and extinguish. We hide or lose our puzzle piece. It frustrates putting the puzzle together.

Our unique gift might be vanquished because we think puzzle pieces are only "spiritual" and useable at a "church service." This kind of thinking manifests itself in a phrase I have heard many times, "The Spirit is not working in our church." The phrase segregates the Spirit's puzzling to an hour on Sunday. The statement reveals an over-emphasis on the more spectacular manifestations of puzzle pieces like speaking in tongues or healing. When people overemphasize the spectacular manifestation of puzzle pieces and locate the weekend service as the main arena where puzzle pieces work, the flame might die out.

Comparison is another reason why the flame of my gift can be extinguished. One day I exercised in a gymnasium. On this particular day I felt strong and moved through the routine in super time. A young man shared the circuit with me. As I glanced at the shoulder apparatus he just used, I noticed that he loaded it with only one block, about eleven pounds. I thought to myself, *What a waste. You might as well not be at the gymnasium. Why do you even bother?* I felt quite superior until I looked at him for the first time and really saw him. He was in a wheelchair.

Whenever I compare myself with someone else, I will either feel superior or inferior. Inferiority extinguishes my flame because I feel I have nothing to offer. This is where Timothy found himself and why Paul admonished him not to be shy.

Superiority makes me unbearable. My gift, amplified through pride and ego, will not bring life to other people—it will be like a flamethrower. Emerson's well-known maxim comes to mind, "What you are shouts so loudly in my ears that I cannot hear what you say."[3]

In Romans Paul admonishes the congregation to have "sober judgment" (Romans 12:3 NRSV). Some of us have to work on our superiority and others on our inferiority. If we fall into the dangerous act of comparison, we will not be able to contribute to the common good. Our task is to work with the grace God gave us.

The division between clergy and laity can also extinguish flames. In recent decades the church has rediscovered the missional nature of God. This is called the *missio Dei*. Because we serve a God who is missional, our churches are an extension of God's sending nature. In the words of the missiologists Stephen Bevans and Roger Schroeder, "the church of Christ does not so much have a mission as the mission of Christ has a church."[4]

One of the beautiful gifts in the missional movement is the rediscovery of every person's puzzle piece as a vital part of God's mission. We are all part of God's mission. All of us are missionaries and in full-time ministry. However, to recapture this beautiful truth we need to unlearn some of our current church practices. One of these is the special privilege we give clergy, full-time ministers and missionaries. We recover our puzzle piece as we realize that in Jesus everyone is a full-time minister and part of God's mission.

The flame is also extinguished when the church is invaded by a consumer mindset and members come with an attitude of perpetual consumption. I have heard numerous references to Sunday church services as "shows." This extinguishes the gift flame.

Jean Vanier, who started the L'Arche movement, comments,

> A community is only truly a body when the majority of its members is making the transition from "the community for myself" to "myself for the community," when each person's heart is opening to all the others, without any exception. This is the move from egoism to love.[5]

The transition Vanier refers to reflects the way we talk about church. Instead of asking, "How was the service?" and then critiquing the songs and sermon, we can ask, "How is my service?" or "How am I a unique gift?"

PURPOSEFUL PUZZLING

The New Testament has beautiful descriptions of the different gifts operating through the church. However, I don't believe these lists are comprehensive. New Testament professor Craig Blomberg concurs:

> The range of functions covered by Paul's various lists of gifts makes it likely that any combination of talents, abilities, and endowments, however suddenly given or leisurely cultivated, may qualify as spiritual gifts, if a believer uses them for God's glory and his work in the world.[6]

In several New Testament passages (Romans 12; 1 Corinthians 12; Ephesians 4; 1 Peter 4) it becomes clear that the purpose of the gifts is toward action and edification within community. The church is not a shopping mall. We use our gifts for the whole. We serve with our puzzle piece.

When we serve with our puzzle piece, we are not merely talking about a particular skill, spiritual gift or talent; we want to focus on the whole person. Overidentifying our gift as only a "spiritual" gift without the accompanying character will lead to reducing people to functions and a devaluing of full personhood. It is about the whole person. More than that, it is about the Giver of the gift. We are building a Jesus puzzle for the good of the world.

DISCOVERING YOUR PUZZLE PIECE

We find clues of our specific puzzle piece through our temperaments. Am I an introvert or an extrovert? Do I focus more on people or more on tasks? We can also look into our passions. What are the topics or areas of life that I can have long and deep conversations about?

Closely related to our passions are our hobbies. Which hobbies do I engage in? Another influence on our puzzle piece is our education. This includes formal and informal education. What am I learning? In which area of my life do I like to learn? Which books or movies stir me? What stories inspire me? These are all pointers to my unique puzzle piece.

One of the most quoted passages in regard to our puzzle piece is the beautiful statement by Frederick Buechner, "The place God calls you to is where your deep gladness and the world's deep hunger meet."[7]

Paradoxically, I think that our puzzle piece also can be influenced by our deepest hurts. Sometimes we can help someone who experiences some of the deep hurt we ourselves went through. The apostle Paul alludes to this when he comments that

All praise to the God and Father of our Master, Jesus the Messiah! Father of all mercy! God of all healing counsel! He comes alongside us when we go through hard times, and before you know it, he brings us alongside someone else who is going through hard times so that we can be there for that person just as God was there for us. (2 Corinthians 1:3-4)

One of the exercises that helped me to discover my puzzle piece was to think of my life story, recounting the highs and the lows and the in-between times. Reviewing your life story might help you understand how your life speaks. Discovering your puzzle piece is just the start, bringing it to the party is the next step, and growing in your puzzle piece follows. By doing this we contribute to the common good.

GROWING AS A GIFT

When I am a gift to someone else, he or she will experience me as a gift. My presence will be helpful. The best gauge of our giftedness is tested within the context of real-life relationships.

Tests are a helpful start in discovering our puzzle piece, but it can't end with the test. Woe to the community that only measures gifts on paper! The best place to discover and develop our puzzle piece is a loving community. The cycle of experimenting and getting feedback on our puzzle piece builds communities. Our gifts usually feel ordinary to us because they come naturally; we need to see ourselves through the eyes of other people.

Acknowledging gifts within a church community is a crucial part of discovering our puzzle pieces. During acknowledgment meetings we can sit at a table and address each individual, starting the sentence with the person's name and naming her or him as a gift: "Christina, you are a gift to me and to our community through your creativity." As we go around the table we acknowledge each other's puzzle pieces.

We can encourage each other to maintain eye contact and to receive the acknowledgments with a simple thank you. Acknowledgment creates spaces where we can become comfortable offering who we are. It is a powerful exercise. Peter Block writes,

> In our attraction to problems, deficiencies, disabilities, and needs, the missing community conversation is about gifts. The only cultural practices that focus on gifts are retirement parties and funerals. We only express gratitude for your gifts when you are on your way out or gone. If we really want to know what gifts

others see in us, we have to wait for our own eulogy, and even then, as the story goes, we will miss it by a few days.[8]

Acknowledgment isn't just uncritical appraise. We also grow when we get balanced feedback. I love the show *Everybody Loves Raymond*. In one of the episodes Raymond, a sports reporter, appears on a television interview. Raymond is excited and his family is all very supportive. This is a once-in-a-lifetime opportunity for him. On the evening of his interview his family are nailed in front of the TV. Raymond absolutely blows the interview; he is pathetic. When he comes home everyone congratulates him on his "excellent" appearance. They don't have the stomach to tell him the truth. Then Raymond contemplates another interview. His father, afraid that this particular puzzle piece will be flung into the world a second time, confronts him with the truth: "I could have eaten a bag of pretzels and farted a better interview than that."

Raymond exercises his puzzle piece in the arena of a television interview and is not a gift to others. Initially he gets fake feedback and then brutal honesty. It is interesting that in the Ephesians 4 passage, as Paul sketches the different puzzle pieces, he writes that "Rather, speaking the truth in love, we are to grow up in every way into him who is the head, into Christ" (Ephesians 4:15 ESV).

When we discover our puzzle gift, we need a mix of love and truth. Imagine a continuum with love on the far left and truth on the far right. All of us are somewhere on this continuum. In the *Raymond* episode his family initially find themselves to the far left. Their concept of love excludes any form of feedback resembling the truth. Raymond's father finds himself on the far right of the continuum; he calls a spade a spade.

Discovering our giftedness happens best when we are surrounded by a truthful love. Ephesians 4:15 almost always surfaces during wedding ceremonies. So does 1 Corinthians 13—the famous passage on love. Using these two passages in a wedding context is definitely not wrong, but it is primarily written for communities discovering their puzzle pieces. As we live out our puzzle pieces, we are invited to be patient, kind and rejoicing. We are also encouraged to bear all things, believe all things, hope all things and endure all things. These beautiful community ingredients help us with puzzle discovering. In the same passage we are warned against envy, boasting, arrogance, rudeness and seeking our own way.

As we puzzle together we are learning how to fit into each other so that we can form a composite picture of Christ. This is a challenge. We can easily become irritable and resentful. Through these puzzle discoveries we are learning the kingdom language of love.

After matriculating I joined a Service Year for Christ team. In the early 1990s these teams were in fashion in South Africa. They consisted of young people giving a year of their lives in order to spread the gospel. It was basically a gap year dedicated to being a gang for goodness. One of our fellow team members was a bit older than the rest of us. As a teenager he ran away from home and lived on the street as a punk and drug dealer.

When he joined our team, all his hair was gone. But he showed us pictures of his pink Mohawk. It was quite impressive. Our friend's unique contribution to the world was his intense passion to share the good news. After one weekend we went to pick him up at his house, but he wasn't there. He had walked to the train station and told people about the love of Jesus. He was brilliant in these one-on-one situations.

As a part of our service year we would often perform dramas or dances and then deliver a talk. Everyone wanted to talk on the microphone. Halfway through the year our friend built up the courage to talk for the first time with a microphone and speakers. His talk was passionate and personal, but his conclusion shocked everyone. He ended his talk staring intensely at the crowd and in typical evangelical style shouted, "And remember God hates sin, and he hates you."

That was not what he meant; he meant to convey the famous line that God hates sin but loves sinners. After telling the shocked crowd what our friend meant, our group had a love-in-truth talk. We commended our friend for his courage and reflected on what happened. Our friend was better in one-on-one situations.

We all have different puzzle pieces.

I have benefited from the love-and-truth talks in my community. These honest conversations help us to be faithful puzzle pieces that beautify the world. Otherwise our communities fall into the perpetual cycle of the preseason *Idol* rehearsals with its biggest blooper reels.

MORE THAN HALLMARK

Beyond the conversation about what gifts occur in this gathering, we each have to deal with the extent that we are bringing the gifts given to us at birth or beyond into the world.[9] When we read the Bible in a copy-and-paste mode, we lift a text out of its context. This method almost always changes the text into a rationalization of the status quo. Jeremiah 29:11 is the quintessential fridge or bookmark verse: "Surely I know the plans I have for you, says the LORD, plans for your welfare and not for harm, to give you a future with hope" (NRSV). When this verse gets lifted out of its context it can easily be used as a rationalization for a comfortable life of wealth or fame. If you have the wrong picture on your puzzle box, this verse—used out of context—can be contorted to justify almost anything. I have even seen it on an expensive sports car bumper!

So let us put this verse back in its original context.

Israel was in exile. They found themselves in Babylon. False prophets rose up telling them everything would be okay. These false prophets proclaimed that Israel's hardships would end soon. Jeremiah writes a letter telling them that they are staying in Babylon—the prophets are misleading them. Here is a part of his letter (it would be good to read the whole passage):

For thus says the LORD of hosts, the God of Israel: Do not let the prophets and the diviners who are among you deceive you, and do not listen to the dreams that they dream, for it is a lie that they are prophesying to you in my name; I did not send them, says the LORD.

For thus says the LORD: Only when Babylon's seventy years are completed will I visit you, and I will fulfill to you my promise and bring you back to this place. For surely I know the plans I have for you, says the LORD, plans for your welfare and not for harm, to give you a future with hope. Then when you call upon me and come and pray to me, I will hear you. When you search for me, you will find me; if you seek me with all your heart. (Jeremiah 29:8-13 NRSV)

The prophets in Babylon had answers to what the good life was. For them it meant a return to Jerusalem. Their dream was safety in a Jewish-only Jerusalem. This was not God's dream. Israel would eventually go back—seventy years later. What were they to do in the seventy years?

Thus says the LORD of hosts, the God of Israel, to all the exiles whom I have sent into exile from Jerusalem to Babylon: Build houses and live in them; plant gardens and eat what they produce. Take wives and have sons and daughters; take wives for your sons, and give your daughters in marriage, that they may bear sons and daughters; multiply there, and do not decrease. But seek the welfare of the city where I have sent you into exile, and pray to the LORD on its behalf, for in its welfare you will find your welfare. (Jeremiah 29:4-7 NRSV)

God challenges Israel to seek the welfare of the city. The Hebrew word for this is *shalom*. It is a beautiful word that drips of fullness, restoration and wholeness. This is what we are to be in this world. We are supposed to live creatively for the welfare of the city. Our collective puzzle pieces become a gift to the world. We are puzzle pieces building a picture of shalom.

We are gifts individually, but we are also a collective gift. If your church is not seeking the welfare of the city, it is not living out its puzzle piece. One of the questions we have to ask repeatedly is, Who will miss our church if we are not in the neighborhood?

I am not wondering how the people in your church would answer this question. What would the people in your community miss? Would the schools, shop owners, businesses and government miss your church if its people vanished from the city? This question is not meant to induce guilt. It is an invitation toward becoming a gift in your city. Are we puzzling the city or neighborhoods we live in?

It is interesting that God's words to these Jewish exiles echoes the mandate in Genesis 1 to be fruitful and multiply. Our job stays the same; we are to make the world a better place. That is our mandate and our invitation. I ask myself, *How can I be a unique gift to the people around me?* Our gang for goodness asks, How can we be a unique gift to the community we find ourselves in?

When we listen to our city we can live into its groans (Romans 8) and become loving presences.[10] We gift the city. The fact that we are gifting the city doesn't come out of our own PR departments. The people in the city tell us. If we don't hear stories of how we have been a gift to the cities and neighborhoods around us, then we probably aren't. We have a wonderful opportunity to live our puzzles in a puzzling way. Peter alludes to this when he notes, "Through thick and thin, keep your hearts at attention, in adoration before Christ, your Master. Be ready to speak up and tell anyone who asks why you're living the way you are, and always with the utmost courtesy" (1 Peter 3:15).

One of my favorite early church puzzling testimonies can be found in the *Epistle to Diognetus*. This letter describes the early followers of Jesus. The author states that the Christians are not sectarian in their manner of living, but there is something unique about them,

> They display to us their wonderful and confessedly striking method
> of life. They dwell in their own countries, but simply as sojourners.
> As citizens, they share in all things with others, and yet endure all
> things as if foreigners. Every foreign land is to them as their native
> country, and every land of their birth as a land of strangers.

Then the author makes this startling claim, "To sum up all in one word—what the soul is in the body, that are Christians in the world."[11]

When we seek the welfare of the city we become the soul of the different geographies we live in. Followers of Jesus become gifts to the people they encounter and the places they find themselves in. This is more than the creation of subcultures where we only communicate to our city with slogans, Christian music, T-shirts and "Turn or Burn" bumper stickers.

As churches we become artisan communities beautifying the city. We bring soul to the city. We become gifts to one another, and our gang of goodness a gift to the city. Together we are built into God's beautiful puzzle, puzzling the places where we live.

Training Naked

FOR REFLECTION AND DISCUSSION

1. How are you a gift?

2. Which gift or personality tests have you already done? Revisit some of the findings.

3. What gifts are you currently withholding from your community? Why?

4. How can you fan your gifts into a warm fire?

5. How are you speaking and receiving the truth in love?

INDIVIDUAL EXERCISE

Take some time (at least an hour) and reflect on your life story. Focus specifically on the ways you have been weaved—your geography, family, education, experiences, passions, hurts and joys. What story is God writing through your life? What do you bring to the party (what have you brought to the party and what do you envision bringing in the future)? Write your thoughts down and schedule some time with your friend(s) to discuss your discoveries.

GROUP EXERCISE

Take some time to honor each other. Look each other in the eye and affirm each other's puzzle pieces ("You are a unique gift to me in the following way . . ."). Then conspire on how you can gift your city in order to move it toward shalom. How can your little band puzzle in your neighborhood or city? Share your puzzling activity on rawspirtuality.org.

SIX

Jesus Moccasins

—◿—

*The ultimate theological foundation for
a missional spirituality is the incarnation, where
Christians continue a similar process where
they contextualize God's presence.*

Roger Helland and Leonard Hjalmarson

I love exploring raw spirituality in wilderness settings. Every year I undertake a wilderness hike with some fellow pilgrims. One year a group of us started at 5 a.m. and ascended the breathtaking four-thousand-foot climb at Monk's Cowl in the Drakensberg, South Africa. It was an arduous 10.6-mile trek. We reached the summit just as the sun set.

One of the men enjoyed the breathtaking scene with intense pain; he had the wrong hiking boots. During the hike his shoes' soles broke off. This meant that he had an almost barefoot experience on the trail. Big blisters formed on his feet. (This was before barefoot running and Vibram's FiveFingers became popular.) It turned the trail into a trial.

I shared in his pain; on the last day I exchanged shoes with him. I walked a day in my friend's shoes. Thankfully it rained all day and I water-walked in the rain-filled footpaths. The group renamed his shoes the "Jesus Water Moccasins."

Moccasins are amazing shoes. They fit like gloves and don't have heels; the sole of the shoe is sown onto the upper part of the shoe almost seamlessly. With these shoes you can feel the terrain. My friend's shoes were only metaphorical moccasins—in reality they gifted me with raw blisters. Raw spirituality connects us to the ground and the blisters of life.

As I follow Jesus, I have the opportunity to walk in his shoes. John, the beloved disciple, tells us that when we abide in Jesus, we walk in the same way he walked (1 John 2:6). Followers of Jesus wear Jesus moccasins. Rabbi Jesus becomes our walk.

Figure 6.1 illustrates Jesus' invitation to walk in other people's shoes. We sometimes refer to the shoes invitation as the incarnational invi-

tation. *Incarnation* is a beautiful theological concept that literally means "in the flesh." In this invitation we ask, Whose shoes am I called into?

Jesus' incarnation signifies that he came in the flesh, or as John tells us, "The Word became flesh and blood, and moved into the neighborhood" (John 1:14).

Figure 6.1

When we talk about the incarnation, we explore how Jesus moved into the neighborhood. Jesus walked in human shoes, our shoes. Jesus wore the moccasins of humanity. He invites us to also practice incarnation. Alan Hirsch explains Jesus' incarnational invitation:

> By living incarnationally we not only model the pattern of humanity set up in the Incarnation but we also create space for mission to take place in organic ways. In this way mission becomes something that "fits" seamlessly into the ordinary rhythms of life, friendships, and community and is thus thoroughly contextualized. Thus these "practices" form a working basis for

genuine incarnational mission. But they also provide us with an entry point into an authentic experience of Jesus and His mission.[1]

When we live an incarnational rhythm we join the Jesus life. Our everyday life becomes a mission of love, not something we do only on outreach events. When we follow in Jesus' footsteps within our daily lives, we put on Jesus moccasins.

As we follow the paths of Jesus in the Gospels, we notice that Jesus' footsteps consistently walk toward the marginalized:

> God's Spirit is on me;
> > he's chosen me to preach the Message of good news to the
> > > poor,
> Sent me to announce pardon to prisoners and
> > recovery of sight to the blind,
> To set the burdened and battered free,
> > to announce, "This is God's year to act!" (Luke 4:18-19)

Slipping into Jesus moccasins is an exploration of the neighborhood, where we discover and learn what it means to be in other people's shoes and notice the marginalized. Our neighbors' shoes challenge us with the questions, Who are my neighbors? and Who are we excluding?

OUR NEIGHBORS AND THE NEIGHBORHOOD

In the two books Luke wrote we find striking examples of Jesus walking in other people's shoes (Gospel of Luke) and how the early church continued that walk (Acts). Luke displays Jesus snapshots that we don't find in the other Gospels. One of Luke's Jesus portraits—the good Samaritan—explores incarnation and neighborhood like no other. It is revolutionary! If your Sunday school recollections of the story don't strike you as revolutionary, then I invite you to rediscover its radical invitation.

Just then a religion scholar stood up with a question to test Jesus. "Teacher, what do I need to do to get eternal life?"

He answered, "What's written in God's Law? How do you interpret it?"

He said, "That you love the Lord your God with all your passion and prayer and muscle and intelligence—and that you love your neighbor as well as you do yourself."

"Good answer!" said Jesus. "Do it and you'll live." (Luke 10:25-28)

Jesus answers the religious scholar's question with a question. And he models the art of asking good questions. The reasons for this art form is that we sometimes perpetuate disobedience by a constant information-seeking loop. Instead of acting on the information we already have, we want to gather more; we become information gluttons.

Jesus interrupts the religious scholar's information loop, reminding him of the truth he already knows, and invites him to personalize it: "How do you interpret it?" (v. 26). Jesus invites the scholar to engage what he already knows—to do it, to put it into practice, "Do it and you'll live" (v. 28). Christ invites the scholar to train naked.

Over the years I have been continually challenged to use the information I already have in a transformational way. I usually don't need more Bible study groups, as good as they are. I need more Bible doing groups. Kierkegaard's warning speaks to me: "God's Word is given in order that you shall act according to it, not that you gain expertise in interpreting it."[2]

Long before Nike's slogan was copyrighted, Jesus invited the scholar to "Just do it!" Training naked stretches us, and more is involved than intellectual debates. However, the religious scholar would rather debate, so he makes a comeback.

Looking for a loophole, he asked, "And just how would you define 'neighbor'?"

Jesus answered by telling a story. "There was once a man traveling from Jerusalem to Jericho. On the way he was attacked by robbers. They took his clothes, beat him up, and went off leaving him half-dead. Luckily, a priest was on his way down the same road, but when he saw him he angled across to the other side. Then a Levite religious man showed up; he also avoided the injured man.

"A Samaritan traveling the road came on him. When he saw the man's condition, his heart went out to him. He gave him first aid, disinfecting and bandaging his wounds. Then he lifted him onto his donkey, led him to an inn, and made him comfortable. In the morning he took out two silver coins and gave them to the innkeeper, saying, 'Take good care of him. If it costs any more, put it on my bill—I'll pay you on my way back.'

"What do you think? Which of the three became a neighbor to the man attacked by robbers?"

"The one who treated him kindly," the religion scholar responded.

Jesus said, "Go and do the same." (Luke 10:30-37)

The scholar would rather discuss the etymology of *neighbor* than be challenged with the weight of a real neighbor. He did not understand that "every person that I meet is a living work of art."[3] He searches for a loophole and wants to justify himself. His intellectual inquiry serves as a butt skin. I also have loopholes that keep me from wearing Jesus moccasins.

A fruitful exercise is to identify all the different justifications or loopholes we use in our lives. In the last few years I have started a rationalization journal documenting all my different butt skins. Discussing my loopholes with friends has been a tremendous help.

Jesus breaks through the scholar's butt skin with a story. Stories disarm us. In the story Jesus explores the neighbor question in a boundary-crossing narrative. Five characters set the main scene. The main characters are a Jew hijacked on the Jericho road, and a Samaritan who encounters him. The robbers, a priest and a Levite play minor roles.

The story confronts the religious scholar with a credible situation—a brutal robbery—within the larger framework of the animosity between Jews and Samaritans. To understand the hate between Jews and Samaritans, listen to two Jewish sayings about the Samaritans. Rabbi Eliezer stated, "He that eats the bread of the Samaritans is like to one who eats the flesh of swine."[4] In the book of Sirach the Samaritans are called "those stupid people living at Shechem" (Sirach 50:25-26). Therefore, given the hate between Jews and Samaritans, the Jews listening to Jesus' story would not think of a Samaritan as someone respectable or desirable. They would expect the hero to be the priest or the Levite, but never the Samaritan!

Yet the priest and Levite walk by—both with sensible justifications for their actions. The Samaritan, however, puts himself in the shoes of the Jewish victim. He slips into Jewish moccasins. What a shocker. It would be like a story of an American soldier who gets ambushed in Afghanistan and is helped by a member of al-Qaeda.

Luke's story is masterful. He says that the priest "was going down that road, and when he saw him he passed by on the other side." The Levite "came to the place and saw him, [and] passed by on the other side." The Samaritan "came to where he was, and when he saw him, he had compassion. He went to him" (ESV). Luke repeats a specific pattern in the story as he draws our attention to proximity, seeing and responding. There is a progression of proximity when he tells the story.[5]

The priest was on the way and the Levite came to the place, but the Samaritan came to where the beaten man was. The priest and Levite move to the other side. The Samaritan moves toward the man.

Incarnation moves us from highways to people. Spirituality for the sake of the world moves us from a detached and abstract "highway life" toward an incarnational rhythm where we walk in the shoes of others. Raw spirituality allows us to learn a compassionate life. Seeing plays a major role in the incarnational life. Where we are and who we spend our time with influences the ways we see and respond.

In the rest of this chapter I will explore these three aspects: location, seeing and responding (LSR). When we follow Jesus into his moccasins we rhythmically engage with our specific location by seeing and responding. It takes place one step at a time. (LSR does not stand for land speed record.)

Because of our South African context I will focus on the neighboring between black and white and rich and poor. I know there are many more boundaries, but I hope these stories will stir you to engage with your own unique opportunities for wearing Jesus moccasins.

LOCATION

I grew up in the South African neighborhood of apartheid—an Afrikaans word meaning "separate." In my neighborhood *our people* were white and mainly rich. *They* were black and mostly poor. In a vacuum of abstraction *they* were generalized as lazy, dumb, thieves and dangerous. We had to protect our people from those people. They became "the other."

This division between them and us was enforced with power. Growing up we breathed the air of racism.[6] South Africa was divided into oppressors and the oppressed. Whites believed they were superior to blacks. I grew up in a white superior bubble that afforded me immense privilege. That was my location.

Bubbles inoculate us from the gifts of diversity. My immunization came from two sources. The first was obvious: apartheid. The second was less obvious: it came from the "homogeneous unit principle" (HUP). It was conceived on the mission fields and transported as a foundational truth for the church growth movement. The following is a description of the heavily debated HUP principle:

The fifth vital sign of a healthy, growing church is that its membership is composed of basically one kind of people. . . . People like to become Christians without crossing racial, linguistic or class barriers. . . . A "homogeneous unit" is simply a group of people who consider each other to be "our kind of people." They have many areas of mutual interest. They share the same culture. They socialize freely. When they are together they are comfortable and they all feel at home.[7]

In the early 1990s HUP was popularly referred to as having a "target market." Churches that use target-market language usually suffer from homogeneity and communities of sameness. This was my neighborhood. It was a place where everyone was more or less the same. Even our shoes looked similar.

However, in South Africa, the homogeneous unit principle was not a new phenomenon. When the Dutch colonized South Africa in 1652, they brought Christianity with them. In the first few centuries the good news seeped into all segments of society. Owners and slaves met together in newly formed churches.

But.

A bubble formed. The homogeneous unit principle took root in a small farmers' community. In 1829, farmers wanted to segregate Sunday worship and specifically the celebration of the Eucharist. These owners didn't want to celebrate the Lord's Supper with their slaves. However, the Dutch Reformed Synod maintained that the Lord's Supper could not be celebrated apart.

But.

The farmers were persistent, and in 1857 they were allowed to meet separately. Walls were erected. The bubble was formed. The decision was worded in the following way:

The Synod considers it desirable and scriptural that our members from the Heathen be received and absorbed into our existing congregations wherever possible; but where this measure, as a result of the weakness of some, impedes the furtherance of the cause of Christ among the Heathen, the congregation from the Heathen, already founded or still to be founded, shall enjoy its Christian privileges in a separate building or institution.[8]

The "weakness of some" became the norm. Farmers and slaves didn't celebrate the Lord's Supper together. A wall was built. A seed for the theological rationalizations of apartheid was sown.

My own homogeneous bubble was formed with the seeds of the church-growth movement's practicalities and the deep-seated feelings of superiority inherited through apartheid.

I don't think South Africa is the only country with a bubble. I have also lived in an American bubble. The world's neighborhoods are still divided into haves and have-nots. Some countries are divided against other countries. When we are confronted with people who are different, we devise all kinds of labeling devices that place *us* in a protective bubble against *them*.

Rich, poor, white, black, brown, male, female, educated, noneducated, old, young, fat, thin, beautiful, ugly, able-bodied, disabled, Christian, non-Christian, gay, straight, married and single. These are only a few of the labels we ascribe to each other on a daily basis. We create groups of *us* and *them*. We create bubbles.

The priest in Luke's story lives in a bubble. While I live in the bubble, I drive through Johannesburg's busy streets and see people who are different than me and go back to "the other side." *They* are a blurry scene through the windshield of my life. The superficial spirituality of the highway is characterized by speed and distance.

Imagine placing a GPS device on your daily life. Where will the imaginary GPS track your daily, weekly and yearly footprints? My GPS revealed that I hung out in immense comfort with people who were just like me. My location was on the other side, in the suburban bubble.

When Jesus moved into his Palestinian neighborhood, he also encountered different bubbles. He navigated them as the gracious bubble breaker. As we read through the Gospels we discovered Jesus' love for diversity. The GPS footprint of Christ shows a rhythm of us-and-them bubble bursting. He embodied this in his own gang for goodness.

When Jesus formed a small group he first invited the fishers Peter, James and John (Mark 1:16-20). Mark tells us that Jesus next invited Matthew, a tax collector (Mark 2:13-17). Matthew most likely had his tollbooth close to where Peter, James and John fished. James and John had the nickname "Sons of Thunder" (Mark 3:17)—they had anger issues. I can imagine how they thundered at Matthew when they had to pay exorbitant taxes on their catch of the day. Jesus nevertheless called Matthew: "Follow me." Can you hear James and John's thunder in response? I imagine them telling Jesus that Matthew didn't fit in "their crowd." Did Jesus really think that Matthew was their target market? They explain to Jesus that fishers and tax collectors don't form Google hangouts.

But that is not all.

Jesus also invited Simon the Zealot into his gang for goodness. Certain zealots were called "people of the dagger."[9] The god of the zealots smiled when they killed those who compromised with the Roman Empire, people like Matthew.

Imagine Matthew's fear when he heard Simon was joining the gang. I picture Matthew telling the group that they need to draw up a group covenant. His first suggestion is, "All weapons stay outside the door." Matthew must have wondered whether the group would be a safe environment for the likes of him.

Jesus brings diverse people together—he places them in the same location. Location plays a major role in incarnation.

When Lollie and I returned from the United States to South Africa, we experienced the location of our birth country in a new way.

Maybe you have also had the experience of leaving your town for vacation, and when you come back you notice new things. Coming back to South Africa gave us new insights. I sometimes refer to it as our conversion to South Africa. When we returned (remember Luke's use of the word?) we moved from the highway—the other side—closer to where the people were. It was eye opening.

SEEING

When Tayla and Liam were toddlers, we taught them the finer arts of communication. One of the sayings in our house is, "Give me your eyes." We remind the kids to make eye contact when we talk to each other. Now that they are becoming older, they are turning the teaching on us. Just the other day Tayla walked into my office and started a conversation with me. My eyes were glued to the computer screen. Tayla gently touched my arm with a certain degree of urgency and said, "Daddy, give me your eyes."

An incarnational life is a process of learning to give our eyes to others. A few years ago we sang a particular song quite often. One of the stanzas states, "Open the eyes of my heart, Lord." Maybe you have also sung this in a church service. What does it mean? Singing songs can easily become part of a disembodied Christianity. God taught me the meaning of opening the eyes of my heart through a precious friendship.

David Mashele joined our gang for goodness early in 2004, and he stood out. When we look at pictures of our community, it is obvious why. He was the only black person in the midst of a sea of whites. Until David courageously visited our community, we were another homogeneous bubble. Even though we studied the rhythms of Jesus and realized God called us to diversity, we were stuck. Thankfully God sent us a good Samaritan, or he was like Cornelius to Peter (Acts 10–11).

David challenged our bubble and became a gift to our community.

David had a specific Sunday rhythm. He drove his car into the parking lot and meticulously cleaned it before the service. He then moved to the community hall where we gathered, entered the toilet and prayed for the service—his petitions echoed from the bathroom floor and ceiling.

One Sunday a family experienced David's "shoes" and initially it upset them. David's car washing on the sabbath didn't strike them as God honoring. They were also troubled because David's loud prayers were not adding to the spiritual atmosphere they expected before a service. They wore David's shoes and decided to pray through their discomfort.

One week later the husband shared that he had to repent because God changed his point of view. He saw things differently. He moved from the highway and the other side to the person. The eyes of his heart were opened. He said he realized that although he had a car that was worth twenty times more than David's, he never washed it: "David's stewardship of his car challenges me. I also realized that I never pray for the service and cannot judge David, who is interceding for our time together."

He stepped into David's shoes, and what happened was unexpected: David became the teacher and this man the pupil. The incarnational life is full of surprises, and God loves to orchestrate role reversals.

I also had a lot of repenting to do, and my own eyes needed to be opened. God used David to recover my eyesight. He became God's answer to opening the eyes of my heart.

One Sunday I felt compelled to get to know David a bit better—I experienced God pressure. I remember that Sunday because it was as if I saw David for the first time. I thought I could help him. Instead, he helped me. I invited my fellow African brother for a meal at a Chinese shop. It was David's first time eating Chinese, and he stumbled through the meal with his chopsticks. When I reflect on my decision to take him for Chinese, I can only laugh at my lack of cultural intelligence. Initiating a friendship through the use of chopsticks was uncomfortable for us. In retrospect I marvel at David's extreme graciousness.

During the meal David told me his story. Incarnation moves us from highways to seeing people and listening to stories, God's and people's. To my shock I found out that David was also a pastor. He faced a challenge that forced him from his rural town to the city. His congregation could not afford to pay his salary. He relocated to Johannesburg to sell fruit at a local market and pastor his congregation from a distance; unbeknown to him, he taught me the fruit of the Spirit.

The incarnational life usually happens best when we are oblivious. Think of those people in Matthew 25 who responded, "Master, what are you talking about? When did we ever see you hungry and feed you, thirsty and give you a drink?" David became Jesus' presence in my life.

David told me about his hometown and his father, brother and sister. He shared with me that he rented a shop where he had a Coke machine, fax and copier, and that he had plans to start an Internet café. It was at this stage that all my anti-kingdom reflexes and folkways kicked in. You see, when I grew up in the bubble, I was catechized into being highly skeptical of the *other*. I was taught that by default people on the other side wanted to take us for a ride. I thought David fabricated the story of the shop. Meanwhile God had a different ride in store for me, the road to recovery. God invited me from the highway toward the beautiful reality of a person.

A few weeks later David phoned me and told me that one of his congregants passed away. He asked me to come to the funeral with him. It was one of those watershed moments. To be totally honest with you, I was scared to death. Because of our segregated past, most white South Africans don't venture into rural areas that are predominantly black.

During the apartheid years we called these black areas "lokasies," an Afrikaans word meaning "location." This was a location whites usually avoided. It was a no-go location. A Caesarea Philippi. I told Lollie about the invitation, and together we decided that I should go—with some other people. Didn't Jesus send out his disciples two by two?

As we drove north on the highway to the province of Limpopo, I was scared and prayed for our safety. In my scarred psyche I battled serious demons of skepticism. It was one of those liminal spaces where you don't know what to expect. Incarnation takes us into these in-between places into other people's shoes.

As we drove into the town of Vleifontein we made our first stop. We saw David's shop with his name painted on the wall. As we live in an incarnational rhythm, we get to know new places and people's names, we move from abstraction to person. We face our skepticism.

"Welcome to my town and my shop," David beckoned. Inside he offered us Coke and showed us his gadgets. A crack emerged in my racist heart. In the movement of incarnation my journey toward wholeness began.

In Vleifontein our hostess was a wonderful woman who opened her house to us in the most amazing way. She slept on the floor so we could have a bed to sleep on. Her story was tragic. A witch doctor poisoned her husband. When he died the witch doctor's family took everything that belonged to her deceased husband and kicked her out on the street. Her embodied hospitality was formed out of this immense pain and suffering. With a beaming smile she told us that she hosted nine women the week before.

I noticed a bunch of stacked up boxes in the corner of her house. My curiosity got the best of me, so I asked her what the purpose of the boxes was. She explained to me that she bought cutlery and extra food every month and placed it in the boxes. Whenever someone's husband dies she walks over with a box. God wastes no hurt. We were slowly slipping into her shoes—they felt like Jesus moccasins. Slowly but surely we moved from the highway to where people were. Our eyes were opening.

Let me tell you another story.

Eddie Ramabulana burst into my life with a prayer request. We were in the same small group at leadership training. The session ended with prayer requests. I turned to Eddie and introduced myself. Eddie is a pastor and lives in one of the informal settlements situated on the outskirts of Johannesburg called Diepsloot.

"Please pray for the safety of our people," Eddie requested.

"There is currently gang initiation in our squatter camp. In order for new gang members to gain access they have to shoot someone from the back of a bakkie [a pickup truck]. Our corrugated iron shacks don't give adequate safety. My congregation is scared."

Eddie inquired what he could pray for my congregation. It was tough. How do you ask a pastor to pray for your overworked parishioners when he shepherds many without work? How do you ask prayers for safe holidays from people who hardly ever feel safe or go on a vacation?

I have been in many prayer circles with pastors, but this was a first for me. I can't remember what my petition was. The incarnational life invites us into a praying life. I slowly slipped into Eddie's shoes—Jesus moccasins. During the next few years we got to know Eddie's community in Diepsloot. Friendships slowly developed. Our eyes opened slowly.

Shortly after returning to South Africa, my friend Schalk invited me to come to Mozambique. Schalk has been an enormous help in understanding what it means to live a life in other people's shoes. He worked with small groups in an all-white church in Johannesburg and followed God into the adventure of relocating to the town of Manica in Mozambique. He was one of eight white people in a town of thirty thousand. In this town Schalk learned new languages—Portuguese and soccer—and he also made a bunch of new friends. He moved from the highway to the people.

So there I was, in the middle of Mozambique, playing a sport that was not my first language. With ten other players on my team I played a ferocious game of soccer; more accurately, they did.

During a short interval in the soccer game I took a sip from my Nalgene bottle. In Colorado everyone had a Nalgene bottle and drank copious amounts of water. My bottle was one of my American artifacts. When I lowered the bottle one of my teammates extended his hand and gestured that he also wanted to take a sip. It was an invitation toward communion—a metaphorical shoe swapping.

In that pregnant moment my segregation sickness kicked in and my stereotypes screamed in protest, *What if he has TB? Cholera? Hepatitis?* In an incarnational instance of clarity I offered the bottle, and the bubble burst. What happened next came as a total surprise. My friend took a small sip and passed the bottle to all the players on the team. All nine of them drank a little. Smiling, my friend said to me, "Here, we left you the last sip."

In that moment I experienced an invitation to a life where abstraction was banned from the field. A Nalgene bottle became a Eucharist invitation. An incarnational space broke open and the floodgates of the kingdom stormed in. I am sure my Mozambican friends don't even remember this, but I do.

As my eyes opened to my unique neighborhood, I realized that there was more to Johannesburg than glitzy shopping malls and comfortable suburbs. Surely, God was also there. But on the margins of Johannesburg Jesus walked in disguise. Slowly but surely I noticed. The question was, how would I respond?

RESPONDING

When we move from the highway toward people, we have the ability to respond. The good Samaritan "came to where he was, and when he saw him, he had compassion" (Luke 10:33 ESV). As our gang moved from the highway of privilege we started seeing people and became friends. Unfortunately, our responses didn't always help. Cultivating a compassionate life takes time and involves making many mistakes.

We have to learn how to do good. The compassionate life is developed.

> Learn to do good.
> Work for justice.
> Help the down-and-out.
> Stand up for the homeless.
> Go to bat for the defenseless. (Isaiah 1:17)

Sometimes our superiority complexes lead to arrogance. We thought we could "do good" without learning. It is this untrained goodness Thoreau reflected on when he wrote, "If I knew for a certainty that a man was coming to my house with the conscious design of doing me good, I should run for my life."[10]

Doing good without learning is a huge mistake and leads to countless hurts. I know, we have made many mistakes and still do. We need to learn how to help without hurting people and ourselves.[11] One of the biggest lessons we learned was that our engagement with other people wasn't a one-way street. We now talk about it like this: "The journey of the rich is to learn that they are not God and have something to receive. The journey of the poor is to learn that they are made in the image of God and have something to give."

The good Samaritan story hints at this dynamic. Jesus tells the story to a Jewish audience. Therefore, the listeners would identify with the victim in the story—a hijacked Jew. This is revolutionary! The Jews are the receiving party, not the givers.

When we always give, we maintain a position of superiority and remain in control. The invitation is to learn to receive. When we become incarnational presences in our neighborhoods, we are not just givers. Sometimes we give like the Samaritan. He gave money, resources and access, and there is a time for that.

Sometimes we receive.

We learn the art of receiving—this is also compassion. The compassion of receiving is an invitation to relinquish power and become weak. Jesus said it is more blessed to give than to receive (Acts 20:35). We also bless others when we allow them to give. In order to help someone regain their humanity, we create a space for them to contribute.

One of the greatest challenges for privileged people is being in positions of weakness and postures of receiving. Henri Nouwen wisely states that "true liberation is freeing people from the bonds that have prevented them from giving their gifts to others. This is true not only for individual people but also—particularly—for certain ethnic, cultural, or marginalized groups."[12]

When we started our relationship with Eddie and the Diepsloot community, we decided that we wouldn't fall into the old charity model where one side always gives and the other side perpetually receives. We wanted a reciprocal relationship. This freaked a lot of us out; it freaked me out too.

When we engage in long-arm charity through short-term projects, long conversations over tea and a meal seem daunting. It is easier to go on a blanket drive than to sit under a blanket while having a conversation. Our inability to have these kinds of relationships forced us to face our own poverty. It leveled the need for healing.

Slowly, friendships formed between us and people outside our bubble.

God used them in our lives and us in their lives. One of the ways we built these friendships is food. Jesus ate communities into being. Raw spirituality develops in the incarnational rhythm of eating good food with God's beautiful and diverse people. It is an invitation to experiment in creating spaces where we can get to know one another and share life together.

At one of our meetings we were an eclectic group of people spanning races and socioeconomic classes. We talked about Jesus and what it means to follow him in South Africa. My wife prepared some muffins and cookies for us. As we drank coffee and tea, we listened to one another's stories and experiences, learning from each other. It was a glorious time.

A few days later I met with Eddie to ask him how his friends experienced the evening.

He told me the story of a woman who joined us that evening. When they got home she approached Eddie and told him how shocked she was to be invited to have coffee and snacks prepared by a white person. "How can I drink from white people's cups?" she asked Eddie.

You see, during apartheid blacks and whites seldom mingled at tables. One of the ways that blacks were reminded of their "inferiority" was through a separate set of cutlery, usually a tin cup and plate. These tools of segregation were stored in a cupboard on the lower level—all of it serving as symbols of oppression. It was a way to communicate that they weren't on the same level as whites.

The woman explained that after she saw Eddie and the others making coffee and drinking from white people's cups with so much liberty, she mustered the courage to follow in their footsteps. She got up and made herself coffee in a "white person's mug." Eddie told me that this lady described this as one of the most liberating moments of her life. She said that she wanted to stay for the rest of the evening!

After this incident I have noticed how many times Jesus used the table and eating as a vehicle for transformation.

LOCATIONS, SEEING AND RESPONDING

Jesus challenges the protective bubbles in our lives. Christ's diverse people challenge the bubbles of our community. Our homogeneous bubbles burst through the appearance of new friends like David and Eddie. As we study the incarnational rhythms of Jesus, we discover that he loves bringing opposites together, reconciling differences.

Men and women, rich and poor, oppressors and oppressed, Jews and Gentiles, healthy and sick—all these people are invited into a movement of love. We are all called into gangs for goodness.

As we rhythmically walk into diverse relationships, our locations change. From these different locations we see differently. Our seeing allows us to respond in reciprocal acts of giving and receiving. We develop a compassionate life.

Within this diversity kingdom mutuality matures. When we follow Jesus in wearing other people's shoes, we make sacrifices. At Claypot we changed our community language from Afrikaans to English. It was an uncomfortable but fruitful process that made our community more accessible. Later, in an effort to further our incarnational leanings, we joined a fantastic organization called Oasis and synchronized our rhythms. We diversified our shoe collection.

I am writing this chapter during the season of Pentecost. During the feast of Pentecost we celebrate the outpouring of God's Spirit, who empowers us to live the adventure of incarnation. When I live in bubble spirituality, I don't need empowerment, all I need is entertainment. Following Christ's incarnational example takes courage and requires empowerment. Before Pentecost Jesus spent forty days with his disciples, teaching them about the kingdom of God. Then Jesus told them, "What you'll get is the Holy Spirit. And when the Holy Spirit comes on you, you will be able to be my witnesses in Jerusalem, all over Judea and Samaria, even to the ends of the world" (Acts 1:8).

It took me very long to understand how threatening this statement must have been for the disciples. When they heard these words they were on a mountain and went back to their Jerusalem bubble. However, God's invitation, coupled with the promise, was that they would move out of their comfort zone—even to engage the Samaritans!

Bursting the bubble takes courage, but the rewards outweigh the sacrifices. I still battle with my privileged bubble—every day. Thankfully I am not alone on this journey. I am part of a gang of goodness. God's Spirit empowers me. God surprises me. Every day brings opportunities to wear Jesus moccasins and grow in intimacy with God. It is incarnation time! Get your Jesus moccasins on.

Training Naked

FOR REFLECTION AND DISCUSSION

1. Imagine that your daily life is tracked with a GPS. What footprint are you leaving? Who are your neighbors?

2. Reflect on your current location (where you live, work or study). What are you seeing? How could you respond?

3. Reflect on an experience when you wore someone else's shoes or someone yours. Share these with your group.

4. Are you more comfortable with giving or receiving?

INDIVIDUAL EXERCISE

Experiment with location, seeing and responding. Ask God to show you someone in whose shoes you can climb (a different culture, religion or background). Read literature and poetry of someone different. Notice what God shows you. When you find someone, listen to his or her story. As far as possible simply listen and ask expanding and clarifying questions. Try not to interrupt with your own opinions and stories, unless the other person asks.

GROUP EXERCISE

As a group design your own group experience. Choose a location you don't often frequent and organize an outing to this place. For example move your meeting from your homes to a place (mall, pub, school, coffee shop) on the other side of the town. As you meet in the new location ask God to open your eyes and help you to move from the highway to the people. Notice what you see, feel and taste, and ask God to help you with your receiving or responding.

SEVEN

Downward Mobility

*Acts of love that resist the world's values involve
the individual believer and the believing
community in downward mobility.*

WARREN CARTER

*Our temptation is to let needs for success,
visibility, and influence dominate our thoughts,
words and actions to such an extent that we are gripped
in the destructive spiral of upward mobility
and thus lose our vocation.*

HENRI NOUWEN

Our culture is obsessed with upgrading. I am consumed by upgrading.
We upgrade our lifestyles, gadgets and games. Some people even
upgrade relationships. Why do we do this? Psychologist Oliver
James calls it the virus of affluenza: "It entails placing a high value
on acquiring money and possessions, looking good in the eyes of
others and wanting to be famous."[1]

Recently a Saudi Prince sued *Forbes* magazine:

Alwaleed, who is often described as the most influential businessman in the Middle East, vowed to sever ties with Forbes in March when its coveted annual Rich List valued him at $20bn—placing him as the 26th most wealthy billionaire on the planet.

The prince insisted he was worth closer to $30bn and accused the respected US magazine of being "demonstrably biased" against Saudi Arabian firms.[2]

Conversely, in the life of Jesus we find a rhythmic engagement with downward mobility. One of the oldest church hymns states, "He who was equal with God emptied himself and became a slave" (Philippians 2:6-7, my paraphrase).

The image of someone running down the ladder (see fig. 7.1) symbolizes Jesus' invitation. With this invitation we ask, *How can I serve with the privileges and resources I have?*

Downward mobility flows out of our decision to keep up with Jesus and not the

Figure 7.1. Downward Mobility

Joneses. When we explore the invitation of downward mobility we discover that God owns everything (Psalm 24:1) and we discover our position as stewards in God's household. We are invited to serve as good stewards in the household of love, where there is enough for everyone.

A PARASITE IN THE INTESTINES

In Luke 12 we discover that the affluenza virus is not a recent development. Luke reports that a man involves Jesus in a conversation on inheritance; he wants more—he has affluenza. Jesus responds with a story.

Speaking to the people, he went on, "Take care! Protect yourself against the least bit of greed. Life is not defined by what you have, even when you have a lot."

Then he told them this story: "The farm of a certain rich man produced a terrific crop. He talked to himself: 'What can I do? My barn isn't big enough for this harvest.' Then he said, 'Here's what I'll do: I'll tear down my barns and build bigger ones. Then I'll gather in all my grain and goods, and I'll say to myself, Self, you've done well! You've got it made and can now retire. Take it easy and have the time of your life!'

"Just then God showed up and said, 'Fool! Tonight you die. And your barnful of goods—who gets it?'

"That's what happens when you fill your barn with Self and not with God." (Luke 12:15-21)

Jesus introduces the story with a warning. Watch out for any kind of greed. Greed wants more. The greed virus is germane in the context of material possessions but can be found in anything, even spiritual things. Some people go from conference to conference seeking the scalps of famous speakers. Jesus warns against all kinds of greed.

When Peter writes his second letter, he describes that some people "have hearts trained in greed" (2 Peter 2:14 NRSV). He uses the same root word for train (*gymnazō*) that Paul uses to urge Timothy to "train yourself in godliness" (1 Timothy 4:7 NRSV). We live in a culture that is deeply trained in greed.

The church is a community that trains toward godliness; the pervasive culture trains toward greed. The church is a gymnasium of grace; the culture is a gymnasium of greed. These two gymnasiums have different goals. Jesus warns us to be on guard. One of the saddest facts is that the church gymnasium often looks just like the culture's training ground. I sometimes find it hard to know which is which.

After the opening warning, Jesus introduces the main character— a rich man. At this point the danger Jesus refers to becomes pertinent. Jesus' followers in affluent societies can easily dismiss the rich man as someone else—not them. Eugene Peterson likens greed to a small parasite in the intestines and notes that "the moment we are wealthy, whether in goods or in God, we are liable to greed."[3]

Jesus warns us to watch out for all forms of greed!

The Lie of the Middle Class

A few months after we returned to South Africa, I sat in a restaurant with my friend Schalk and said, "I just want to figure out how to follow Jesus as a middle-class white South African."

Without missing a beat Schalk responded, "Well, you can start by not lying to yourself."

I was a bit bemused and asked him to explain.

"You are not middle class," he said. "We are both rich."

Talk about training naked!

Schalk spoke the truth in love (Ephesians 4:15)! And his speaking exposed my butt skin. I hid behind the butt skin of the philosophical term *middle class*. My hiding was subconsciously strategic. By not identifying with the poor or the rich I placed myself in a no-man's land. It was a safe place where I didn't have to take a stand. The lie of the middle class is the ideal incubator for the greed parasite. It turned out that I had an intestine problem!

With a greed-infested intestine I read Scriptures like Luke 12, which addressed rich people, and transferred the attention to those "other people" who live in the rich neighborhoods on the hill—or in America. I insulated myself. The lie of the middle class gave me a safe place where I comfortably enjoyed my privilege while I criticized the rich. In this mode I can bash the Saudi prince without examining my own upward tendencies.

That restaurant moment helped me; it moved me from the gymnasium of greed to the training grounds of grace.

After Schalk's loving rebuke I researched the median income in South Africa and found that I earned way above it. I realized that I wasn't middle class but rich. I discovered a website called global richlist.com, where a person can see the place of his or her income in terms of the world's population. It was quite a shocker for me.

But this journey was not an individual one. With our friends we embarked on the joyful and arduous journey of downward mobility. We printed out all the Bible verses written to rich people and allowed them to become our gymnasium apparatus. This opened a whole new journey for us.

On one leg of our journey we discovered the early church's radical engagement with downward mobility. With many other churches we wanted to recover something of the early church's vibrancy. So we researched the first three decades of the church's downward mobility and dialogued with what they taught.

During the research I conducted eighty interviews with people in suburban Johannesburg churches. One research question was, "How would you describe yourself in socioeconomic terms?" Only two people described themselves as rich, and the rest said they were middle class or average. It was surreal to conduct interviews in million-dollar homes where the owners described their financial position as "only middle class" and said they "have worked hard" for their money.

The lie of being middle class is one of the major butt skins facing affluent churches. It is this lie that keeps the parasite of greed alive and well. When I identify myself as middle class, I can always compare upwards—the people above me become my point of reference.

I AND OUR

The Luke 12 story narrates what we might call "The Life of I." The rich man's life revolves around himself. Until God interrupts his self-referential life, the rich man is wrapped in a monologue. The words *I* and *me* isolate him. He uses it eleven times. He is a man on his own.

Kenneth Bailey notes how pitiful it is for a person in Israel to achieve success and have only himself or herself as a dialogue partner.

Raw spirituality moves us toward community. Spirituality suffocates in monologues.[4]

Greed isolates *I* from *our*; it cuts off. A journey upward is characterized with ever-growing layers of isolation. When I live with greed, other people become competitors instead of companions. Raw spirituality trains us downward and outward.

The Luke 12 rich man's incessant inward focus is in stark contrast with the prayer Jesus taught his disciples.

In the early 1990s it became a fad to replace all the collective words in prayers and songs with the personal pronoun *I* or first person possessive *my*. Pastors would encourage congregants to exchange "For God so loved the world" with "For God so loved me." The Lord's Prayer became, "My father who art in heaven" followed with "give me my daily bread."

This personalization of the text is a perfect symptom of the hyperindividualism of our age. This individualized spirituality facilitated my journey of becoming the Luke 12 rich man.

The personal pronoun *I* is definitely included and implied in the collective *our* of the Lord's prayer, but when I change it to *me* or *I*, I can easily leave the collective out. Ridding my life of the greed parasite meant detoxing from individualized versions of the Lord's Prayer. Cyprian, one of the church fathers, diagnosed this same sickness. He wrote,

> Before all things, the Teacher of peace and Master of unity did not wish prayer to be offered individually and privately as one would pray only for himself when he prays. We do not say: 'My Father, who art in heaven,' nor 'Give me this day my bread,' nor does each one ask that only his debt be forgiven him and that he be led not into temptation and that he be delivered from evil for himself alone. Our prayer is public and common, and when we pray, we pray not for one but for the whole people, because we, the whole people, are one.[5]

So I started an exploration into who the *our* in the Lord's Prayer included when I prayed. I trained away from the abstract, from saying, "When I pray this prayer I carry the world in my heart," with a Thomas Merton-like pose. Away from Dostoyevsky's wonderful line in *The Brothers Karamazov*, "I love humanity, but I wonder at myself. The more I love humanity in general, the less I love man in particular."[6]

I wrote down names of actual people—my own prayer genealogy. As I reviewed my list I was shocked to find out that it included a very small and selective group of people. Moreover, I was jarred by the fact that my little group's lifestyles strained mostly in an upward direction and included no one "over there." Our little group was far removed from praying for "daily bread." We lived in a world where our needs advanced beyond three meals a day.

A certain question haunts me. How are we formed when the "our" of my community is constituted by people who are constantly up-grading their lifestyles? Within an upwardly mobile community the effects of consumerism and capitalism seep in on a regular basis. The worst aspect of this is that I am so prone to rationalize this lifestyle. I sometimes think that I hang out with people just like me because we become justifications for each other's lifestyles. Henri Nouwen echoes this: "My whole life I have been surrounded by well-meaning encouragement to go 'higher up,' and the most-used argument was: 'You can do so much good there, for so many people.' But these voices calling me to upward mobility are completely absent from the Gospel."[7]

I sometimes feel that the affluent church is more like a medical insurance group than the gang for goodness we are supposed to be. Whenever someone joins a medical insurance or "medical aid," as it is called in South Africa, the person goes through screenings to make sure he or she is not a high-risk member. Medical insurers walk a fine line when it comes to members. They have actuaries that work tirelessly to calculate the medians, determining who is allowed in and who is not.

By congregating with fellow upwardly mobile congregants we ignore those at the bottom—they are too high risk for us. The sad reality is that we miss Jesus in our risk aversion. This kind of church sociology is not new. James wrote in his epistle,

> My dear friends, don't let public opinion influence how you live out our glorious, Christ-originated faith. If a man enters your church wearing an expensive suit, and a street person wearing rags comes in right after him, and you say to the man in the suit, "Sit here, sir; this is the best seat in the house!" and either ignore the street person or say, "Better sit here in the back row," haven't you segregated God's children and proved that you are judges who can't be trusted?
>
> Listen, dear friends. Isn't it clear by now that God operates quite differently? He chose the world's down-and-out as the kingdom's first citizens, with full rights and privileges. This kingdom is promised to anyone who loves God. (James 2:1-6)

The danger of upward mobility is that I am cut off from the marginalized and miss out on the kingdom life. When upwardly mobile people connect with fellow yuppies, they disconnect from the poor among them and develop unhealthy desires that blur the line between needs and wants.

That is one of the reasons why the invitation to be in other people's shoes is so important. As we develop friendships with those wearing different shoes, it challenges our upwardly mobile lives.

DON'T CUT THE CORNERS

When Jesus told the Luke 12 story, the rich man's self-referential life would strike the audience, but there is something else. His stinginess. In Leviticus, God instructs landowners to work with their booming crops in a peculiar way.

When you harvest your land, don't harvest right up to the edges of your field or gather the gleanings from the harvest. Don't strip your vineyard bare or go back and pick up the fallen grapes. Leave them for the poor and the foreigner. I am GOD, your God. (Leviticus 19:9-10)

God invited landowners to provide for others out of their surplus. But the rich man wants everything; he desires more for himself. In isolation he shapes his investment toward his ever-shrinking *our*. He has no regard for other people; he is not praying "give us our daily bread" but "let me build it bigger." The Steins note that if the rich man paid attention to the good Samaritan story he would have said, "And I shall be even more able to serve God and those less fortunate than I!"[8]

As his life shrinks, his soul shrivels.

The downward journey is best practiced in conjunction with the shoes of incarnation rhythm. These two are interwoven. When I stand in the shoes of people that are different from me, especially in terms of socioeconomics, I am invited to move downwardly.

Does this mean that I am never allowed to enjoy anything? Of course we can enjoy ourselves, but when it becomes our main aim we move into the Luke 12 man's shoes. This narrative is marked by the insatiable desire to always eat, take it easy and be merry.

When I grew up in Johannesburg my dad occasionally took us to a restaurant. It was a highlight for my brothers and me. I now frequent restaurants on a weekly basis, and I have upgraded the kinds of restaurants that I see as special. My desires morph—they upgrade.

Is it wrong to celebrate with loved ones in a restaurant? No. Is there room in my life for moderation and giving up restaurant trips so that others can enjoy daily bread? Yes. This is a modern interpretation of the Leviticus 19 text and can be applied to buying cars, coffee, snacks, gadgets and many other material things.

Paul's advice to Timothy remains relevant:

Tell those rich in this world's wealth to quit being so full of themselves and so obsessed with money, which is here today and gone tomorrow. Tell them to go after God, who piles on all the riches we could ever manage—to do good, to be rich in helping others, to be extravagantly generous. If they do that, they'll build a treasury that will last, gaining life that is truly life. (1 Timothy 6:17-19)

As I determine what my needs are, I engage in the wonderful adventure of becoming rich toward God.

PRAYING FOR OUR DAILY BREAD

As we researched the early church's engagement with faith and wealth, we discovered that these followers of Jesus operated with a foundational assumption: Christians will distinguish between their needs and wants. They interpreted the "daily bread" in the Lord's Prayer as a reference to the everyday needs of Jesus' followers. In these communities they determined their needs and shared their surplus with one another so that there "was not a needy person among them" (Acts 4:34 NRSV).

I have always been fascinated by the contemporary church's vocal desire to return to the Acts 2 church. Talk about returning to this kind of church usually ignores the fact that they had all things in common and sold their possessions and belongings to distribute the proceeds to the needy.

One of the oldest treatises on the topic of faith and wealth was penned by Clement of Alexandria, who explored the question, Who is the rich man to be saved? In those early centuries, followers of Jesus wondered if people like me, rich people, could be saved. This tells us something about their commitment to downward mobility.

In one of Clement's other writings, *The Instructor*, he comments on Luke 12:

Those concerned for their salvation should take this as their first principle, that all property is ours to use and every possession is for the sake of self-sufficiency, which anyone can acquire by a few things. They who rejoice in the holdings in their storehouses are foolish in their greed. "He that hath earned wages," Scripture reminds us, "puts them into a bag with holes" (Haggai 1:6). Such is the man who gathers and stores up his harvest, for by not sharing his wealth with anyone, he becomes worse off.[9]

Clement makes a distinction between possessions that are used and those that are held. He encourages congregants to figure out what they really need and then critiques a lifestyle of hording. Surplus is not for hoarding but for giving away. This is a tough word, but also a freeing invitation.

In another passage Clement notes that God gives property and possessions for our use and needs, not for showing off. Therefore, as we determine our needs we have to keep in mind that "expensiveness should not be the goal in objects whose purpose is usefulness. Why? Tell me, does a knife refuse to cut if it be not studded with silver or have a handle of ivory?"[10]

Clement even challenged rich congregants who use gold toilets:

It is a farce, and a thing to make one laugh outright, for men to bring in silver urinals and crystal vases . . . , and for silly rich women to get gold toilets for excrements made; so that being rich, they cannot even ease themselves except in superb way. I would that in their whole life they deemed gold fit for dung.[11]

With Clement as our downward mobility conversation partner, news broke in the United States of a prominent ministry leader who owned a "commode with a marble top" worth $23,000.[12] It seemed that times haven't changed that much. However, we had to deal with our own greedy parasites.

We wondered what it means to ask for our daily bread. In his small catechism Luther asks: "What is meant by daily bread?" He answers,

> everything that nourishes our body and meets its needs, such as: Food, drink, clothing, shoes, house, yard, fields, cattle, money, possessions, a devout spouse, devout children, devout employees, devout and faithful rulers, good government, good weather, peace, health, discipline, honor, good friends, faithful neighbors and other things like these.[13]

He interprets "daily bread" as support for and wants of the body and contextualizes needs for his specific time. It became clear to us that we had to distinguish between needs and wants within our own context too.

We explored the questions, What do I/we really need, and what are wants or luxuries? It was life-giving to figure out what we really needed within our community's specific context. We became convinced that in the absence of actively exploring our needs and wants we would automatically move upward and increase our standard of living.

I suggest that Jesus followers have the needs and wants conversation at least on a yearly basis. We have found the introspective season of Lent helpful. Scheduling this exploration is crucial. As we grapple with our needs and wants, we ask for God's perspective on our daily bread. We work through the nitty-gritty of our budgets and expenses. This process brings a lot of freedom. Not engaging in this process leaves us with gnawing feelings of guilt that can paralyze.

When Paul wrote to the Corinthian church he distinguished between bread money and seed money. Bread money goes toward needs. Seed money goes to others. I find this a helpful way to explore the needs and wants conversation (2 Corinthians 9:10).

One of the phrases we heard continually when we engaged in the process of determining our daily bread is "Needs and wants are relative." That is absolutely true. Vocation, career, season of life, geography, life stage and a myriad of other factors influence needs and wants. This is a fact of life. But it cannot be used to evade this important question and its exploration in the lives of Jesus followers. The question is, What is your *relative* daily bread? It demands a personal answer. Yes, it is different for every person.

If my *our* is populated with my own biological family, then our daily bread will be determined in relation to my family's unique makeup. However, if my *our* extends and envelopes other brothers and sisters, then the needs will become relativized by these additional relations. Our relationships determine our needs.

Determining my needs in the context of friendships with David, Eddie and my Mozambican friends challenges the luxuries I might indulge in if those relationships are not there. Giving up a TV upgrade might become an opportunity for someone's education. "Give us our daily bread" then becomes an invitation to think broader than my life alone.

CHURCH FINANCES

When families and individuals wrestle with the invitation of downward mobility, it has implications for the church too. On a communal level we reimagine the ways we work with God's money entrusted to the church. This has huge implications for the finance committees of churches.

In most of the churches I have served, the finance team is composed of highly successful businessmen and businesswomen. These wonderful folk know all the ins-and-outs of the financial system. They bring tremendous expertise and skill in building bigger barns for corporations. But a challenge is embedded in this. If we don't listen to Jesus' warning in Luke 12, the financial acumen of these teams might derail churches from a downward journey of trust, risk and obedience.

When churches don't have to pray for daily bread, we can easily build false securities into our lives. Greed becomes a parasite in the intestines of the church. When we work with finances there's always tension between "sound business principles" and "crazy, God-inspired giving." Greed usually camouflages itself in the language of safety and security.

One weekend we had a finance team meeting scheduled at our house. As the members arrived, I ushered them into one of their SUVs and took them on a road trip. As we drove it became clear to them that we were headed to one of our local squatter camps, which is only fifteen minutes from my house. The particular squatter camp has close to 100,000 people living in an area of slightly more than one square mile. This freaked the stewardship group out. They wanted to know why we were going there. Was it safe?

I explained to them that we couldn't afford the luxury of managing God's money in isolation. I tried to explain that we were in grave danger of imagining an economy that excludes the people around our posh neighborhoods. The team understood our challenge. As we stopped the owner of the SUV hesitantly asked, "What if they steal my car?" Our stewardship meeting became an embodied exploration of our *our* and our levels of trust.

It was a glorious afternoon as we walked among the sacred ground of our neighbors' lives. We concluded our pilgrimage and entered a little shebeen, "an unlicensed establishment or private house selling alcoholic liquor and typically regarded as slightly disreputable."[14]

Our host asked us if we wanted some beer. We all nodded. We live in Africa, and a walkabout like this makes one thirsty! As he stood in line to buy beers, the group engaged in whispered conversations on how we would repay him. One of our accountants did the math.

To our surprise he arrived with one bottle of beer instead of five. Smiling he opened the bottle, took a sip and passed it on. The bottle was circulated between us, and we all took a sip. In the corner, next to our table, a lone man was sitting. He was invited into the community. The bottle went around the circle twice.

When we offered to pay our host back, he looked offended and told us that the beer was his gift. Our gift to him was to receive. As we travel a downward journey we step into the fabric of a giving and receiving community. We partake in a kingdom weaving in which we are formed into new patterns of belonging.

Our day out had a huge influence on the way we imagine the money God gives us and how we "work the budget." For one, we don't store up tons of money in a bank account for a rainy day. God's people need that money. We learned that the early church called this kind of hoarding "theft from the poor."[15]

We also learned that everything belongs to God. Many stewardship teachings start from the false premise that we have to give 10 percent. The implied assumption is that 90 percent belongs to us. We moved the conversation away from asking people to give 10 percent to asking God how much of God's resources they may keep.

WILD SPACES

In order to travel on a downward journey we train new reflexes. Jesus calls it being "rich toward God" and contrasts it with our old reflex of laying up treasures for the self (Luke 12:21). New reflexes open wild spaces. The Ugandan theologian Emmanuel Katongole borrows the idea of wild spaces from Sally McFague. A wild space is "whatever does not fit the stereotypical human being or the definition of the good life as defined by conventional culture."[16] As we engage in wild spaces we ask questions of the norms and imagine new possibilities.[17]

When we create wild spaces we don't build bigger barns but boisterously share God's good provisions. Instead of living the upward life, we create cracks in the system. These cracks become escape hatches to a different kind of life in which we serve with what we have—a wild kingdom of God space. Let's explore a few reflexes of questioning and imagining that can lead to wild spaces.

From exclamation to questions. Our materialistic society has a natural Wow! response when someone builds a bigger house, buys a new car or upgrades a gadget. In unison we exclaim, "Wow! That is amazing." What would happen if we preceded the upgrading or buying with a process in which we ask Why? We exchange the *wow* for an inquiring and discerning *why*.

"Why do you need a bigger house, more expensive car or exciting new upgrade?"

The question is not condemnatory but inviting. There might be good reasons for buying, building and upgrading. However, we need to beware of all kinds of greed. Rationalizations abound! The *why* question opens the possibility for a wild space where we align our stuff with a kingdom narrative. It connects *my* stuff with *our* bread.

Recently, good friends of ours explored the why question within our community. They are amazing, hospitable people who live in a cramped space. So they are considering the purchase of a bigger house. As we explored the why question, they clearly articulated their heart for hospitality. Within their life story it makes sense to upgrade. They explored the why.

As we explore the why question, it uncovers the possibility for an exploration of our desires. In William Cavanaugh's insightful book *Being Consumed*, he comments that "humans need a community of virtue in which to learn to desire rightly."[18] Investigating our desires invites us to increasingly interweave desire with God's desires. When we sing the song "This is my desire, to honor you," I sometimes stop and ask if it's true. Is it my desire to honor God with my stuff? Most of the time that particular worship song questions my real desires. If the answer is no, then it becomes an opportunity to move toward a new wild space.

I want to desire rightly.
Sometimes.
I am not there yet.[19]
But I am on the way.

Instead of a rationalizing "wow" community, churches can become wild spaces where we encourage each other to move from our selfish needs toward the life-giving desires of our good and generous God.[20]

Richard Foster offers helpful principles that can be seen as clearing the ground for wild space, from moving from an automatic wow to a why.

1. Buy things for their usefulness, not their status.

2. Reject anything that is producing an addiction in you.

3. Develop a habit of giving things away.

4. Refuse to be propagandized by the custodians of modern gadgetry.

5. Learn to enjoy things without owning them.

6. Develop a deeper appreciation of creation.

7. Look with healthy skepticism at all "buy now, pay later" schemes.

8. Obey Jesus' instructions about plain, honest speech.

9. Reject anything that breeds the oppression of others.

10. Shun anything that distracts you from seeking first the kingdom of God.[21]

Imagining with other people. When Clement of Alexandria wrote his treatise *Who Is the Rich Man That Will Be Saved?* he noted that the challenge of wealth is that it creates desires within rich people that run contrary to God. Clement concludes in his treatise that these inbred passions won't be eradicated at once. Downward mobility is a lifelong process.[22] Clement suggests to those who are pompous, powerful and rich (that is me), "find a man of God to set over yourself as a trainer and mentor."[23]

Followers of Jesus need financial planners who rhyme us in the rhythms of God's kingdom economics. These financial planners live with a different imagination. They help us to invest in heavenly treasures. Clement continues,

Have godly respect for someone—even if it's only for one
man. Answer to someone—even if it's only to one man. Learn
to listen to someone else, though there may be only one other
man who speaks candidly to you. His words may be harsh,
but they will bring healing. For your eyes should not continue unrestrained. It is good for them to sometimes weep
and hurt. This will bring you greater health in the long run.
Likewise, nothing is more detrimental to the soul than un-
interrupted pleasure.[24]

Clement knew that rich people have the means to buy themselves
an alternative reality. We need help. I need help. Clement invites
followers of Jesus who are addicted to upward mobility to share
their everyday budget with at least one other person. Can you
imagine that?

Over the years I have asked many followers of Jesus whether they
feel comfortable sharing their Jesus journey with a group of intimates.
The answer is almost always yes. Christians love sharing their faith.
When I ask them if they are willing to share their salaries and budgets
with the same intimates, I usually encounter huge resistance. This is
a damning commentary on our real treasures.

Over the years we started small groups in which we opened our
budgets to one another. These groups are totally voluntary, and it
obviously takes immense trust. That is why Clement states that we
cannot do this with many people. During these budget-sharing
meetings we lovingly explore ways that we can create wild spaces
within our everyday financial lives.

The purpose is an edifying exploration, not a pointing finger of
condemnation. These loving friendships have helped many in our
community to engage with downward mobility. In some of these
groups couples have embarked on the journey to see how much of
their resources they can give away. One couple determined that their

lifestyle could be attained on 20 percent of their monthly income; they are giving the rest away. The journey and groups became grace-empowered spaces of freedom.

Recently, a businessman told me that it gives him great joy to know that 80 percent of his work time brings bread to other people. It helps him when he is working with a difficult client or faces frustrations at work. He is brilliant with "making money," and as his *our* enlarged it connected him with a greater adventure—with the life that is truly life (1 Timothy 6:19). His life is embedded in a bigger story.

Downward mobility is the means to a bigger end. The purpose of downward mobility is a connection with God's bigger household story. Bigger barns are boring.

Imagining a different economy. The word *economy* comes from two Greek words that literally mean "the management of the household."[25] As my household expands beyond selfish needs and bigger barns, it creates a bigger imagination. Downward mobility enlarges the way we pray for "our daily bread."

Churches can become the answer to the "our daily bread" prayer in terms of housing, buying transport, meals, furthering education, funeral costs and many creative versions of daily bread.

In the new household of God we celebrate the fact that all things belong to God, not just 10 percent. This means that we have the wonderful privilege of being stewards in God's new economy. The cars we drive, the homes we live in, the educations we have—all of it belongs to God.

Corrie ten Boom's timeless advice helps us to explore wild spaces: "Hold everything in your hands lightly, otherwise it hurts when God pries your fingers open."[26] Slowly but surely we are freed of the ways our possessions possess us. We also loosen the grip we have on our stuff. We learn the ancient Christian dictum that "goods have been given to us so that we can do good."[27]

Jesus is our example in the downward mobility journey. The best song ever written on the downward journey is in the book of Philippians:

> Think of yourselves the way Christ Jesus thought of himself. He
> had equal status with God but didn't think so much of himself
> that he had to cling to the advantages of that status no matter
> what. Not at all. When the time came, he set aside the privileges
> of deity and took on the status of a slave, became *human*! Having
> become human, he stayed human. It was an incredibly humbling
> process. He didn't claim special privileges. Instead, he lived a
> selfless, obedient life and then died a selfless, obedient death—
> and the worst kind of death at that—a crucifixion.
>
> Because of that obedience, God lifted him high and honored
> him far beyond anyone or anything, ever, so that all created
> beings in heaven and on earth—even those long ago dead and
> buried—will bow in worship before this Jesus Christ, and call
> out in praise that he is the Master of all, to the glorious honor
> of God the Father. (Philippians 2:5-11)

Training Naked

FOR REFLECTION AND DISCUSSION

1. How would you describe yourself in socioeconomic terms?

2. Visit the site www.globalrichlist.com and reflect on your place in
   the worldwide household. How do you feel about your place?

3. What are your needs and wants?

4. Write down the name of the people you pray for in the "give us
   our daily bread" prayer. How do these people influence your needs
   and wants?

5. How do you feel about sharing your daily budget with someone
   you trust?

INDIVIDUAL EXERCISE

Create stickers for yourself that say "Mine" and "God's." Then use them to label the possessions in your house. It reveals which possessions possess us.

GROUP EXERCISE

Do a spring cleaning of your house. Identify items that you don't use that could benefit others. No Jesus junk (stuff that is broken). If you are brave, invite a friend to help you to identify extras and doubles. Gather as friends and brainstorm how you can create wild spaces through this downward journey.

EIGHT

Working It Out

*Vocation or calling is about much more than what we do.
It is one person—God—calling to another person—me.
Cooperating with God, growing in him for the
sake of others, is our singular vocation, no
matter what we do to get a paycheck.*

Todd Hunter

This chapter is for those who are working in full-time ministry. *But* before you skip it, read the next few paragraphs.

I sometimes ask the Sunday service congregations if there are any full-time ministers in attendance. Sometimes one or two people raise their hands. By the end of the teaching I ask the question again. If all of the people don't raise their hands I have failed in teaching them a vital part of a raw spirituality and a crucial truth retrieved by the Reformation. We are all part of God's mission. All Christians are in full-time ministry. Through our everyday lives we become good infections in the world.[1]

Another way to state this is, every Christian is in full-time ministry. By the end of this chapter I hope you will embrace the exciting journey of joining God's mission through the work you do.

Many Christians divorce their 9-to-5 jobs from their with-God life. This is ironic since there is a huge awakening in the business world to the importance of spirituality in the workplace. When our discipleship with Jesus is not connected to our working lives, we effectively cut God out of the biggest chunk of our lives.

In figure 8.1 the clock symbol represents our 9-to-5 lives, and this rhythm engages the question, How can I work out my salvation in my job, ministry, work and life?

The invitation to "work it out" helps us to move into our role as full-time ministers, wherever we are. It reconnects our 9-to-5 activities with the overall arc of a Jesus-following life. The *work it out* phrase can be found in the letter Paul wrote to the Philippians:

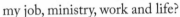

Figure 8.1

> Therefore, my beloved, just as you have always obeyed me, not only in my presence, but much more now in my absence, work out your own salvation with fear and trembling; for it is God who is at work in you, enabling you both to will and to work for his good pleasure. (Philippians 2:12-13 NRSV)

With the invitation to work it out we allow salvation to seep through all areas of our lives. A salvation-saturated life breaks through our human dichotomies between sacred and secular, allowing our jobs to become arenas for training in godliness.

CAREER TO VOCATION

We live in a culture that places a premium on what our job is. Think of how we engage in initial conversations with others. They often start with the question, "What do you do?" We often equate worth in relation to the kinds of jobs people do. Let me use an *I* statement for that. I often reduce people to their function. I often confuse people's job descriptions for their identity as image-bearing children of God.

When Lollie and I moved to Colorado, I met Gordon, introduced myself and asked, "So, what do you do?" He responded, "Why don't you rather ask, Who are you?"

It was a valuable moment of speaking the truth in love. What we do in our jobs cannot capture who we are. We are more than our job descriptions. Who we are is infinitely more complex than our jobs.

Yet what we do influences who we are and who we are becoming. It is true that our jobs sculpt our lives and influence who we become. But we are more than our jobs. Just think of Jesus. Would we reduce him to his job? Can you imagine meeting Jesus and thinking he is just a carpenter?

When we answer the question What do you do? we sometimes mix up three words that mean quite different things. These words are *job*, *career* and *vocation*. In different communities these words have different meanings.

Jobs are linked to specific activities or tasks that can be crossed off a list. Eugene Peterson gives a helpful definition of jobs: "Jobs have job descriptions. A job is an assignment to do work that can be quantified and evaluated. It is pretty easy to decide whether a job has been completed or not. It is pretty easy to tell whether a job is done well or badly."[2]

A career is usually associated with a commitment to a specific profession. Someone who is trained in medicine develops a career in the field of medicine. The word *career* signifies how someone develops within his or her occupation over a long period of time. A career consists of the accumulation of jobs.

The word *vocation* comes from the Latin *vocare* and means "call." If I ask South Africans, "What is your vocation?" A large part of the hearers will hear the question as "When did you receive your calling to work for the church?" Vocation or calling is associated with professionally paid ministers or clergy.

This is unfortunate and something that the Reformers challenged with the concept of the priesthood of all believers. When Martin Luther encountered Christians who didn't think they had a vocation—a call—he quipped, "How can you think you are not called?" and said that the reduction of vocation to the clergy

> is without doubt the worst trick of the devil. How could the devil have led us more effectively astray than by the narrow conception that service to God takes place only in the church and by works done therein. . . . The whole world could abound with services to the Lord, not only in churches but also in the home, kitchen, workshop, field.[3]

As we explore the "work it out" rhythm, we want to recover a sense of vocation and full-time ministry that includes more than just the clergy. In Jesus we are all called. As we follow Jesus we are invited to discover and develop in our vocation. We ask, *How is Jesus calling me to live within my unique circumstances in my job and career?*

This is a journey of aligning jobs and careers with the discernment of vocation. When jobs and career lose their mooring from vocation, or link to a misguided vocation, our lives go astray. A career without a sense of vocation becomes senseless.

Harvard psychologist James Waldroop explains that the word *career* "comes originally from the Latin word for cart and later from the Middle French word for racetrack. In other words, you go around and around really fast for a long time—but you never get anywhere."[4]

We "work it out" when we moor our jobs and career to vocation. Without a sense of vocation a career can become a senseless racetrack with no other purpose than making money. We call this "careerism." This making of money for money's sake saps all energy and leaves career-o-holics depleted—it deafens the call.

When someone is caught in the racetrack of career, he or she might be promoted, which means more money. But such a person only exchanges a small racetrack for a bigger one. The job becomes bigger and saps the energy out of the rest of life. Life careens out of control. The racetrack never connects with the bigger life journey. Career becomes redemptive when it connects with vocation. If people can still celebrate with someone after a distinguished career, we would say that the person probably lived out a vocation.

As we work it out, we move from career to vocation. Our job becomes part of a bigger story. If people are good at making money, it becomes vocational when they connect to the bigger story of God. Some people are called to make money in order to give it away—lavishly.

When we engage our jobs and careers vocationally, we do what we do to the glory of God (1 Corinthians 10:31). Martin Luther explained that someone sweeping the kitchen is living out his or her vocation as much as the monk praying. He also cautioned against a shallow version of vocation where we sprinkle Jesus' name on our doings or display little crosses on our creations. "God is interested in good craftsmanship."[5]

Vocation calls out in all areas of our lives. Dallas Willard and Bill Heatley give a helpful description of possibilities (see fig. 8.2).

Figure 8.2. Circle of Vocation

The smallest circle is your career with its job description. It is what you do to earn money. It is where you spend your proverbial 9-to-5. If my whole life collapses into this circle, it becomes my all-encompassing reality. All my thinking and speaking revolves around my job. My job will squash me into a one-dimensional person—careerism careening into chaos. It will sap all my resources and leave me depleted.

Some people enjoy vocational satisfaction in the career and jobs they perform. If we can't experience it in our jobs, we can still do our job to the best of our ability—as if we do it to the Lord. This is what it means to do all things in the name of Jesus (Colossians 3:17). If our jobs don't give us vocational satisfaction, we can still work out our calling in other areas of our lives. This is hopeful for those who don't have paid jobs.

The next circle represents ministry. It links with the unique puzzle piece you represent and the ways that God wants you to serve humanity with your unique contribution. Your ministry is how you embody God's goodness serving the world. It is how you are blessed to be a blessing. Dallas Willard describes it as "that part of God's work he has entrusted to you. There are some things that God specifically wants done in your time and in your place, and He's given those things to you to do."[6]

Next is your work, which is "the total amount of good that you will accomplish in your lifetime. For many of us, our family will be a large part of that. I say that because in being Christ's person in the world today, we need to make sure that we don't sacrifice our family to our ministry or job."[7]

This is a refreshing redefinition of work. When I restrict work to my job and career (what I get paid to do), then I cut out large chunks of my life. Some of our best work might happen outside the place where we receive a salary. Just think of the mother teaching her daughter how to handle rejection. Is it work? Yes! Is it vocational? Yes!

Then there is the life circle that includes how we play, hang out with others, relax, eat and engage with whatever we do to glorify God.

God is interested in the person we are becoming through our career, ministry, work and life.

As we "work it out" and move toward vocation, we discern God's voice in our life, work, ministry and job/career. Keeping these different layers in mind helps. The different circles can build on each other. My job can include my ministry and become my life's work. But there will also be work I do which I don't get paid for that is part of the legacy I am leaving. Just think of parenting, married life and friendships. We also have a life outside of ministry and job duties.

As we "work it out" we discern our calling. Every person is living out a certain calling. We are listening to a voice. The question is which voice(s) are we listening to?

When I worked as a student pastor, I convened small groups at the University of Johannesburg. I love working with college students. Their honesty and inquiring minds stir me. One of the small groups was filled with prospective accountants. When I asked them why they wanted to become accountants, all of them had a predictable answer: "I want to make lots of money." They were listening to the call of mammon.

These students were not to blame. When I sat down with them, it became apparent that they were raised in families who placed the call of financial success and security above any other voice. They equated success with wealth and collapsed all of life into a shallow category of net worth. They were on their way to drowning in their jobs or joining the rat race—careerism. Thankfully we have beautiful Christ-following accountants who can show the way out of this senseless race. Any career can become a vocation when it is seen as part of God's calling to serve him and make the world a better place, when it becomes part of God's mission to serve others.

GOD DIGS OUR DIRT

Followers of Jesus follow a working Jesus. Jesus engaged in work and modeled his own life on his Father's work: "Jesus answered them, 'My Father is still working, and I also am working'" (John 5:17 NRSV).

Work was God's idea. When we meet God in the opening scenes of Genesis, we find God with soiled hands. God is the potter. This was a shocking alternative to the pictures of God painted by non-Israelites. Their gods didn't demean themselves by working with their hands. That was beneath them.

We serve a God who digs dirt.

The God revealed in the sweat and teardrops of Jesus artfully creates. We join God who creates us as his workmanship so that we can also join in becoming blessings who beautify the world. We serve a God who enjoys work. In the opening paragraphs of Genesis the phrase "and God saw that it was good" cascades in pleasurable refrains. God digs good work.

In the Philippians 2 passage where we find the phrase *work it out*, Paul paints two beautiful pictures of God. "Be energetic in your life of salvation, reverent and sensitive before God. That energy is *God's* energy, an energy deep within you, God himself willing and working at what will give him the most pleasure" (Philippians 2:12-13).

Paul first paints God as "the One who works mightily."[8] Then he draws a picture of God delighting in our work. God digs our dirt. Paul reminds the Philippians that the "working out" they do, like the Genesis work, produces pleasure in the God who works mightily.

We engage in our everyday work in the gymnasium of grace, with our God looking on with pleasure. This "working it out" is done with *fear and trembling*. Paul is the only New Testament author who uses this phrase (1 Corinthians 2:3; 2 Corinthians 7:15; Ephesians 6:5). In the Ephesians passage he describes a certain kind of working it out: "Slaves, obey your earthly masters with fear and trembling, in singleness of heart, as you obey Christ; not only while being watched, and in order to please them, but as slaves of Christ, doing the will of God from the heart" (Ephesians 6:5-6 NRSV).

As we work it out we engage in our work with fear and trembling, not because we are afraid of any earthly boss but because of our deep respect for God. We respect God when we align our jobs and careers with the God who watches us with a pleasurable eye.

Unfortunately many earthly bosses receive more fear and trembling than the God who created us. When we realize that God is our boss, we are invited into a journey of "working it out" to the pleasure of God.

SHINING LIKE STARS

The initiating step in seeing my career as a vocation is to acknowledge God as my primary boss. Whatever job or career I follow, I do it in the presence of God and for his pleasure. Followers of Jesus report daily in the employment of God. Our job description is to please God. When God becomes my boss, I listen to a different voice.

My friend Gerrit is a good example of this. As a newly married man he made a commitment to his wife that he would not allow his job to overwhelm the rest of his life and specifically not his relationship with Tina. He understood that his marriage and family are part of his work. One Sunday morning his boss phoned and told him that he needed to come in urgently. Gerrit said no. It was the weekend, and he was with his family. It took guts. Gerrit listened to a different boss. He listened to God.

On Monday his boss asked Gerrit how he would have responded if he forced him to come in. Gerrit replied that he would have resigned. His boss responded that he was glad he didn't force Gerrit. He valued the work Gerrit did.

In Philippians Paul writes, "Do all things without murmuring and arguing, so that you may be blameless and innocent, children of God without blemish in the midst of a crooked and perverse generation, in which you shine like stars in the world" (Philippians 2:14-15 NRSV). As we "work it out" we shine. Something about our life is different. We do what we do energized by God. Our work is beautiful. It gets noticed. My friend's boss understood that Gerrit's career was part of a much larger whole.

I know our work is not always smooth sailing. We might lose our jobs in order to maintain our vocation. Sometimes our job is difficult. The Genesis narrative gives an apt description of the frustrations of work: "you'll be working in pain all your life long" (Genesis 3:17).

When sin entered the world, work became a struggle. In Genesis 3:18 we read that Adam would work among thorns and thistles. Work is not cursed, but it is difficult. Sometimes our work clicks in place with the bigger story of God; other times it is a battle.

We live as people under construction in a world that is being reconstructed. All creative acts involve struggle. But the struggling is not in vain. God is working to make all things new. God's followers work it out, energized in a different way. Our work is not in vain; it echoes toward eternity.

How do we shine our lights at work? There are many answers to this question. We can choose a career that furthers social justice in the world. Or we can do a job in such an honest and skillful way that people wonder at our work ethic and start asking questions. This might open opportunities for relationships and Jesus conversations. Some people choose careers so they can influence culture through changing policies in politics, economics or education. Many people choose careers that make the world beautiful. Other people see their career as a way to earn great amounts of money so they can give it to people and organizations that make a kingdom difference.[9] The options are endless. However, it will take discernment to understand how to faithfully live out our vocation in a specific career.

LEARNING FROM THE NORTH AFRICANS

In the early church, followers of Jesus took decisions about job, ministry, work and life pretty seriously. If someone entered the fellowship of the committed and practiced a job that was crushing his or her soul, the church encouraged the person to quit. If someone engaged in a job that damaged the earth or scarred other people, he or she was called to resign. In one of the early documents this process is explained: "The professions and trades of those who are going to be accepted into the community must be examined. The nature and type of each must be established."[10]

These early followers took the time to discern which careers were helpful to the kingdom. The document goes on to explain in painful detail which professions were allowed and which were rejected. One of the careers that the early church rejected was acting. In contrast to our Christian culture's excitement when celebrities accept Christ and use their platform for him, the early church asked actor converts to resign. They felt that the platform would corrupt the convert's journey because he or she would build a profession in pretense.

In the third-century North African city of Thena, an actor quit his job when he became a Christian. He stopped acting himself but established an acting academy. Euchratius, the actor's pastor, wrote to his mentor Cyprian to ask his advice. Was it okay for the ex-actor to teach new actors? Cyprian responded that the actor turned actor-teacher had to resign again! But Cyprian told Euchratius that they (as a church community) should support the actor on his pilgrimage to a different job and career. They helped him out through the church's offering.[11]

These early followers were serious in their commitment to "working it out"; they were willing to put their money where their mouth was. If someone transitioned out of a soul-crushing job, they supported the person emotionally and financially, and thereby became a new kind of family. If the church becomes serious about vocation, we also will have to put our money where are mouths are.

In 2006 one of our friends sensed that her job was not glorifying God. Suzette took the courageous step toward rediscovering her vocation and recovering her authentic self. This meant that she resigned from a high-paying job. Her resignation had huge financial implications and challenged her trust levels. Would she trust God to look after her, and would her community support her as the North African Christians in the third century supported the actor?

Suzette's eighteen-month sabbatical was a practical move toward developing a healthier "work it out" rhythm. Her sabbatical was influenced by several factors. First, the job demands placed on her meant that she spent almost all her time and energy "making money for other people"—all of her energy was dispersed into the job circle.

Second, she wanted to explore the other circles. Suzette has a wonderful servant's heart and a passion for development work. So she explored this with our friends in Mozambique. On top of this she reconnected with her initial calling as a nurse. She also facilitated wheelchair tennis for the South African Tennis Association. She has a desire to help people who live with passion and spirit despite the hurdles they face. Third, she felt that she needed some discernment on her future life in Johannesburg.

As Suzette took her sabbatical, her church community opened their hearts, homes and wallets. As she lived with a few families, she discovered that discerning a vocation is not a solo affair. Suzette's courageous journey became a wonderful irritant within her community and stirred many on to ask the "work it out" questions themselves. When Suzette reflects on her sabbatical and what she learned, she says,

> I am still unpacking some of the lessons that were anchored during my sabbatical. I realized the importance of understanding how my job fits into God's overall plan for my life. I regularly ask myself, *What do I do with what I am learning and earning at my work?* I continue to unpack the foundational truth that I am more than my job description. My sabbatical also taught me the importance of Shema (listening) and exploring the tension between a being and doing life.

Suzette didn't run away from her job in veiled idleness. She carefully planned her sabbatical and left her former career responsibly. Even though her job was unsatisfactory, she allowed her external circumstances to become a gymnasium for growth. When I think of Suzette's journey, I am reminded of James' instruction,

> Consider it a sheer gift, friends, when tests and challenges come at you from all sides. You know that under pressure, your faith-life is forced into the open and shows its true colors. So don't try to get out of anything prematurely. Let it do its work so you become mature and well-developed, not deficient in any way. (James 1:2-4)

SABBATH PAUSES

So how do we discover our vocation? Should all of us take a radical step like Suzette? Discovering our vocation cannot be cultivated at the speed of light. John Ortberg tells of a phone conversation with Dallas Willard when he moved from California to Chicago. John asked Dallas what he could do to live a vocational life. Dallas replied, "You must ruthlessly eliminate hurry from your life." John eagerly wrote the advice down and asked, "What else is there?" Dallas paused and repeated, "There is nothing else. You must ruthlessly eliminate hurry from your life."[12]

We live in a culture that makes busyness our business. But we are called to press the pause button and slow down. We cannot listen to the voice of God in a hurry. The classic disciplines for pausing are sabbath, solitude and silence. Pausing allows us to reassess the direction our career, ministry, work and life are taking. It allows some perspective. During these pauses we reflect on how the rhythms of our lives line up with the voice of the One who calls us "beloved." It gives space to ask, *How am I working it out?*

In Exodus 20:8-11 we are taught that we take sabbath because God also rested after his work. In this rest we recover our first calling, which is always to a relationship with God (1 Corinthians 1:9). We live into this vocational invitation as we stop and pray. We plug in with God.

Like Suzette, we recover what it means to be a human being before a human doing. Eugene Peterson explains, "The work/rest rhythm is built into the very structure of God's interpenetration of reality. The precedent to quit doing and simply be is divine. Sabbath-keeping is commanded so that we internalize the being that matures out of doing."[13]

In Deuteronomy 5:15 we find another reason why sabbath is important. As slaves Israelites never had a day off. This turned them, persons made in the image of God, into utilities. They became workers and slaves: "human resources." We keep sabbath to recover our humanity and to preserve the humanity of others. Whenever we partake in communities that take sabbath rest seriously, we reconnect with each other as created in the image of God. The moment we begin to see others in terms of what they can *do* rather than who they *are*, we mutilate humanity and violate community.[14]

In the absence of a sabbath rhythm, with the corporations I start to believe that I am primarily a human resource. Subsequently, I look at others in terms of their functionality. Sabbath helps us to dethrone dehumanizing practices in the workplace. It unmasks language used to control us, such as the word *deadline*. (I know of no one who died of failing to meet an unrealistic deadline.)

As a follower of Christ I stop in order to celebrate that I am not a slave. I am a friend of Jesus. As a friend of Jesus I regularly pray and play. As we pray we attend to God's voice. When we play we explore our humanity and recover the adventurous kingdom life of love. Sabbath creates a reflective space wherein we synchronize with God enjoying beauty; we harmonize with the resting, happy God who delights in his creatures.[15]

The art of sabbath is simple. Schedule a day when you pray and play. For many followers of Jesus, Saturday or Sunday could provide the perfect day. But any day can suffice. The important thing is to schedule the day. Each person will play and pray differently. Traditionally, followers of Jesus prayed together at the Sunday church service and then played afterward. Unfortunately, some people lost the art of playing, and Sunday sabbaths became somber and sober affairs. When I grew up, Sundays were serious days—no-sport days—and church days were silent.

On my sabbath I pray, read and spend some time in creation. When I am outside, I reconnect with the bigger story of our Creator and recreate. Some of my friends exercise sabbath through

- walking
- biking
- gardening
- painting
- baking
- love making
- playing with pets
- eating outside
- preparing fresh meals
- camping
- companionship
- sport

You can experiment with your own list. Whatever you do, do it in a spirit of playful leisure. Richard Foster reminds us that the church fathers encouraged *otium sanctum*, "holy leisure."[16] Holy leisure is a time to get back into a God rhythm, which helps us to reconnect with our vocation.

Book your sabbath in your calendar with the words *otium sanctum*. When someone asks you to do something during that time, respond that you have a very important meeting scheduled. I assure you that most of the time people won't ask questions. The calendar is god in our culture. If they insist on knowing—tell them you are busy with the serious job of *otium sanctum*.

As I engage with sabbath rhythms I reconnect to the good and beautiful God who calls me his beloved. We are God's beloved and live in the unshakable kingdom of God. This is our identity and place.[17]

As Paul exhorts the Philippians to "work it out," he reminds them that God is also at work in them. We are not alone. God is with us. With a loving community we discover the vocation of our lives. Our vocations are a million reflections of God's love shining into the world. We embody formation for the sake of the world.

Some church communities find it helpful to gather in groups of people with similar jobs. They explore how to creatively live out their vocations within their careers. What does it look like to do the full-time ministry of a teacher, engineer or lawyer? One of my friends regularly ordains different professions during their Sunday gatherings. He ends the service praying for different professions, sending them out as full-time ministers "working it out" for the pleasure of God.

"Working it out" is the process of discovering our vocation. As we discover our vocation we learn what it means to synchronize our working lives within the story of the kingdom of God. Thankfully we are not alone; God energizes us and works in us. We are created to engage this working out. May you "work it out" as a full-time minister!

Training Naked

FOR REFLECTION AND DISCUSSION

1. How do you feel about the statement that all Christians are called into full-time ministry?

2. How do you currently feel about the circles of job, ministry, work and life?

3. What does hope look like within your job place?

4. What work is God calling you to?

5. Which sabbath practices have you found helpful?

6. Ask your family and friends what they think the impact of your job is on your life, or what they think your calling is.

INDIVIDUAL EXERCISE

Set aside a special time in nature and think about the person you were made to be. Think about yourself as an older person, fully alive. Now, draw up your weekly schedule, and work out what you spend the most hours on. What would you need to add or take away in order to become the person God is calling you to be?

GROUP EXERCISE

Get together with some friends and explore what it would mean for you to moor your job and career to a vocation. It might be helpful to gather with friends that have the same occupation. Get a group of teachers, engineers, psychologists or other professions together and brainstorm ways you can baptize your professions.

NINE

Learning Jesus

He that made us without ourselves,
will not save us without ourselves.

AUGUSTINE

All habits and practices are ultimately trying to make us into a
certain kind of person. So one of the most important questions
we need to ask is: Just what kind of person is this habit
or practice trying to produce, and to what
end is such a practice aimed?

JAMES K. A. SMITH

When Liam was five he wanted to learn karate. So I took him to a local *dojo*—meaning "the place of the way." I decided to sit in on the class to see what the sensei, a "person born before another" or "teacher," would impart into my precious son.

The sensei was an impressive man with rows of badges on his karate clothes. He looked masterly. He took his pupils through a stretching routine that showed off the children's flexibility. As I watched them, my mirror neurons fired and I cringed with pain imagining how I would do splits like these kids. As the stretching concluded the class split in two.

Unfortunately, the sensei gave the little ones over to one of his apprentices. The trainee opened the class of novices with the following scenario: "What would you do if you are walking down the street with your mommy and a man wants to knife you?"

Liam's eyes widened like two UFOs. This scenario didn't compute well with his five-year-old experience. For the rest of the class the aspirant sensei taught the little kids how to turn a knife back on an assailant.

It was not my brightest parenting moment.

As we drove home, Liam and I reflected on his experience and he voiced his distaste. "I don't want to knife anyone, Dad!"

Back home Liam went to his room, closed the door and started sobbing. It was the kind of crying that heaves the whole body in swells of sorrow. When Lollie arrived home, we walked into the room. After Liam calmed down he confided in us through his sobs, "Can I wear karate clothes and the cool colored belt without training in karate?"

Liam desired karate clothes without karate training.

My experience with Liam got me thinking about Christianity and what it means to be a Christian. Many people want Jesus clothes, but not the training. Many people have bad associations with training in Jesus. Some had a bad experience with a would-be teacher. Or maybe they were never introduced to a body of learning that was helpful in training them. When we told some of our friends about Liam's experience, they encouraged us to come to their *dojo*, which will give him a more wholesome experience. We will see.

Jesus once said that when a disciple "is fully trained [he] will be like his teacher" (Luke 6:40 ESV). When I desire Jesus' clothes, I am invited to train in Jesus' *dojo*.[1] The church contains within its history an immense treasure chest of what it means to train in Jesus. This training is the art of discipleship.

DISCIPLESHIP

When the apostle Paul explored with the Ephesian community what it means to be clothed with Jesus, he contrasted their old life with the new (Ephesians 4:20-24). He reminded the Ephesians that they "learned Christ" in a specific way. This learning took place as they acquired new rhythms and unlearned destructive practices (4:17). As disciples we root our lives in Jesus (Colossians 2:7), we unlearn old ways of being human and habituate ourselves anew. Paul said to the Corinthians, "Be imitators of me, as I am of Christ" (1 Corinthians 11:1 NRSV).

In the early church imitating Christ was an exciting journey of learning Jesus. This embodied learning included beliefs and practices. In our culture we place huge emphasis on the importance of the cognitive aspects of discipleship. We tend to view people, as James K. A. Smith says, as brains on sticks.[2] However, we are far more than brains. We are holistic and embodied people. Therefore, discipleship takes place in all aspects of our lives. When we engage in raw spirituality we follow Jesus with our whole being. This includes our head but also the rest of us. Jesus referred to this when he invited us to love him with our heart, strength, mind and soul, and to love our neighbor as ourselves. Disciples desire to imitate the lifestyle of their rabbi, not just parrot his teachings.

The invitation of holistic embodiment is a lifelong journey. When Paul wrote to the Thessalonian disciples, he urged them toward a long obedience in the same direction: "We ask you—*urge* is more like it—that you keep on doing what we told you to do to please God, not in a dogged religious plod, but in a living, spirited dance. You know the guidelines we laid out for you from the Master Jesus" (1 Thessalonians 4:1).

Through Jesus' life, death and resurrection we have been reconciled with God. We have been justified. The sacraments of baptism and Eucharist remind us of our incorporation into the trinitarian God— we are part of the spirited dance. Through the Spirit's empowerment our practices and habits form us into specific people. We are being sanctified. As we learn Jesus, we synchronize our daily rhythms with God's amazing grace. The word *disciple* means learner. As disciples we become lifelong learners of the Jesus life. As I learn Jesus, I face my current reality and continue to enroll as a disciple in the school of Jesus. This is the process of training naked.

SPIRITUAL KINETICS

My friend Walter is a biokineticist. In his vocation he assesses the movement or rhythms of bodies (bios) and prescribes exercises to strengthen and rehabilitate movement (kinetics). When Walter assessed my movements (kinesthetics), he observed my body rhythms. As I placed my body through different paces, he asked me questions about my training and daily habits. He also explored previous injuries. Have I sustained any body traumas? Did I experience any bad training experiences (like Liam)? Walter looked at my flexibility and observed me as I performed motions with my body. He also followed me in the gymnasium as I performed exercises on the equipment. As I lifted weights, he stood next to me and gave me instructions on how to optimize some of my movements.

As I reflect on my time with Walter I am reminded of what Paul had in mind when he used the Greek word *gymnazō* (train) in 1 Timothy 4:7-8. As Walter assessed the movements of my life, I metaphorically enacted the naked part of "training naked." Training starts from our current reality and develops from that reality.

After the assessment phase Walter helped me with the training part of "training naked." On a weekly basis Walter sent me a program that prescribed specific training exercises. Every set of exercises started with twenty minutes of warmup. I confess that as I started the new training program I was wasted after the intro! After the warmups I was given a mixture of familiar exercises and new ones I had to learn. The idea is to have a mixture of familiar and unfamiliar training methods. Crunches I knew, but burpees were new (and not the same as belching).

I received a training program every week, and as I engaged the training I logged my performance. Every second week I would take my weight and body measurements. As I gave feedback, Walter adjusted the program for the next week. Within this dynamic system, there was nowhere for me to hide my progress. I trained naked.

Throughout this book we have trained toward the development of raw spirituality. In this last chapter I am going to assume the role of a biokineticist, of sorts. In order for you to continue with the development of raw spirituality, we are going to work on the two aspects Walter helped me with. We are going to face our current reality, that is, become naked in the training naked process. Then we are going to work on the training part in the training naked process.

EXAMEN TO IDENTIFY TRAINING NEEDS

Whenever we start a new exercise or regime, we usually fill out a form with our current eating and exercise habits. This is not a shaming exercise but a way of gauging our current reality. As we develop raw spirituality with a rhythm of life, we also review our current rhythms.

An ancient practice that helps us with a rhythm review is the prayer of examen. It is a prayer developed by Ignatius of Loyola in the sixteenth century. St. Ignatius is famous for his *Spiritual Exercises*. During the exercises Ignatius wanted to help trainees to discern their daily rhythms and to discern where they wanted to go. Like Walter, who monitored the movements of my body, Ignatius wanted his followers to determine the movements of their daily lives. It was his response to Socrates' dictum "The unexamined life is not worth living."

In his helpful book on Ignatian spirituality, *Journey with Jesus*, Larry Warner explains the basic movements of the examen prayer.[3] The following is an adapted version of the prayer. First, give thanks to God for the period you are examining. It usually consists of the past day, but you can make it longer. Second, ask God to reveal to you where your rhythms have been helpful and where they diverted you from God, where have you adopted conscious or unconscious rhythms that moved you toward and away from life. Third, examine your words, thoughts and deeds during the past day. Fourth, confess your sins and ask for God's forgiveness. Fifth, ask God to give you grace so that you can live in sync with the Father, Son and Holy Spirit in the following day.

As you progress with the development of raw spirituality, I suggest incorporating a regular examen to determine where your rhythms are currently taking you. Take at least a week, preferably two, to determine your current rhythm. It is also helpful to remember the season of life you are in. A student's rhythm will look different from a new mom's. A retiree will have a different rhythm from a teenager. As you discern your current rhythms, the following questions might be helpful.

- What are some of the most substantial rhythms in your daily life?

- Which rhythms take most of your time? What kind of person are you becoming as you move in them?

- Which rhythms are currently helping you to learn Jesus?

- Which rhythms are currently hindering you from learning Jesus?

- What are some of the rhythms you and your companions can engage in to love God and others?

- What role does a church service play in your conception of rhythms?

Contextualizing to Determine a Training Program

Once you have explored your current rhythms, it is time to determine a rhythm that will be life-giving and enable you to learn—and clothe yourself with Jesus. As we explored raw spirituality in this book, we looked at seven rhythms represented by different symbols (see fig. 1.1 in the introduction).

To determine the rhythms, we explored the life of Jesus, of which the Gospels are our primary source. We asked, What did Jesus teach? How did Jesus live? Or, What rhythms will help us to become disciples of Jesus? These rhythms are variations on loving God and others with heart, soul, mind and strength. They serve as headings under which we can place several of Jesus' invitations to follow him. The headings are like major muscle groups that we exercise in the gym (e.g., shoulders, chest and legs).

Once we determined the rhythms, we chose culturally relevant symbols for each one. When this book's rhythm of life was contextualized for the mission organization Oasis, they changed a few of the rhythms and symbols (see fig. 9.1). I tell this story so that you can get a feel of how the contextualization takes place.

Figure 9.1. Oasis rhythm of Life

Most of the Oasis staff live in the marginalized areas of Johannesburg. Some of them live in squatter camps. As they encountered the rhythm of life, they changed the first symbol (#1) with a mirror,

because they had negative connotations with being counted and the capitalistic drive of "being number 1." The mirror symbol (see fig. 9.2) helped them to engage with their image of God and pictures they have of themselves.

They also changed the bread-and-wine symbol to a pot—an African symbol for community (see fig. 9.3). In some of the

Figure 9.2

communities they work in, wine is still a controversial issue—but everyone knows the three-legged pot.

As they engaged the downward mobility rhythm, they reflected that most of them are already down and wondered whether they should go down even further. They agreed that Jesus teaches us servanthood and stewardship, but didn't resonate

Figure 9.3

with the downward symbol. They also didn't resonate with the shoes symbol. As they read through the Gospels they also added an extra rhythm.

Oasis replaced the shoe with a tree symbol and a circle symbol (see figs. 9.4 and 9.5). The tree invites people into a journey of imagining what it would look like to see God's kingdom come in the neighborhoods where they are planted. The circle is called the circle of inclusion and explores who we are including and excluding.

Figure 9.4

Oasis added a rhythm with a medical bag (see fig. 9.6). South Africa has one of the highest HIV/AIDS rates in the world. Our country also suffers from huge emotional scars. The rhythm of the medical bag explores the healing ministry of Jesus, and journeys with the question, In what area of my life do I need wholeness? The Oasis South Africa rhythm is now contextualized in the different countries where Oasis works. In Oasis Belgium, where the staff comes alongside women who are traf-

Figure 9.5

ficked from Thailand into Europe, they changed the community symbol to a rice cake, which speaks to the Thai people.

Another way to contextualize the rhythm is to work from your local church's vision and mission to design a rhythm that will help you to embody the vision within the congregation's daily rhythms.

During the course of this book we explored every rhythm through four movements of learning. We explored theological *input* through Bible passages and stories. We searched with *questions* linked to the specific rhythm. Then we trained with an *exercise* gathered within

Figure 9.6

the cadences of a *community* of encouragement. These movements of learning (input, questions, exercises and community) attempt to develop an embodied spirituality that leads to engagement with the world.

I propose that the four movements of learning form the backbone of the continual development of raw spirituality. Once you have determined your current rhythms, as well as your preferred rhythm of life and its symbols, you can work on these four movements.

Input or Curriculum

Whenever you are thinking about starting a new exercise or diet regime, you will find an incredible amount information available to help you out. Bookstores have sections dedicated to these topics, not to mention the Internet. It is the same in the church. Every Sunday millions of Christians receive new teaching. Some hear two sermons on one day. Then, during the week, thousands of podcasts give easy access to some of the most breathtaking theological input available since the dawn of time.

Most local churches have a steady stream of good teaching and preaching flowing into their communal life. (There are exceptions, of course.) On top of that, we have virtual and brick-and-mortar bookstores with volumes of teaching. We are not starved for information.

However, despite the immense theological input available, we face some challenges. One maxim illustrates this: "We are educated well above our level of obedience." This is a huge challenge for developing raw spirituality. There is an enormous need for maintaining a healthy hearing-and-doing balance.

The Oxford-based Jesuit scholar William Harmless tells the story of how a man sought out the desert father Theodore of Pherme to obtain a teaching from him. For three days he begged the abba to give him a word. Theodore didn't give the man a teaching; he refrained from the microphone and didn't publish a podcast. So the man left. Theodore's disciple asked the leader why he didn't give the man a word. The old man replied, "I did not speak to him, for he is a trafficker who seeks to glorify himself through the words of others."[4]

In this information-overload culture we might confuse spirituality with the incessant greediness for reading the latest book or hearing the most profound sermon or lecture. We might become traffickers in spirituality. When Jesus told the parable of the sower, he used the image of different kinds of soil. Jesus concluded the parable with a challenge: "Are you listening to this? Really listening?" (Matthew 13:9).

We are invited to carefully journey with the information we are entrusted with. In another context Jesus said, "Then pay attention to how you listen; for to those who have, more will be given; and from those who do not have, even what they seem to have will be taken away" (Luke 8:18 NRSV).

One of the ways we can pay attention is to protect the seeds we have been entrusted with. Journaling can help us to pay attention to how we listen. By writing down some of the seeds that God drops onto my path, I pay attention. Another way to deal with the information deluge is to use your rhythm of life sketch as a way to organize different seeds. We can file books, sermons, lectures and other life-giving input around the different rhythms.

Under the #1 rhythm we might file information helping us to paint a healthy picture of God. The plug symbol is for connections with God, like the different spiritual disciplines. Beneath the bread-and-wine rhythm we organize community-related inputs like family matters, friendships and conflict. As we catalog things beneath the different rhythms, we make sure that we pay attention to the seeds that have been entrusted to us. We also map inputs that helped other communities (see an example at rawspirituality.org).

It might also help to diversify our inputs from a wide variety of God's family, including the different traditions and denominations within the church at large. (Renovaré's streams are helpful here—contemplative, charismatic, social justice, holiness, evangelical, sacramental—and also people from different geographies, like reading books from South Africans.)

As we engage with inputs from people who are different from us, we gain something of Paul's Ephesian prayer, "And I ask him that with both feet planted firmly on love, you'll be able to take in with all followers of Jesus the extravagant dimensions of Christ's love. Reach out and experience the breadth! Test its length! Plumb the depths! Rise to the heights! Live full lives, full in the fullness of God" (Ephesians 3:18-19).

Many churches will benefit by cataloging what they already have in a rhythm schema so that the congregations can have access to the seeds that have been scattered in the past. Determining your current rhythms, contextualizing a preferred rhythm and cataloging your inputs prepare the ground for the training part of training naked. Once we have these concepts in place, we move on to questions and exercises.

QUESTIONS

As we become more like Jesus we learn the art of asking good questions. Jesus asks questions, good questions, unnerving questions, realigning questions, transforming questions.[5] Some versions of spiritual formation are built on the myth that all we need is the right answers, and that the answers have to come easily. Fill-in-the-blank spirituality might be great for parrots, but it won't form a person into the fullness of Jesus. The Franciscan Richard Rohr states that "easy answers instead of hard questions allow us to try to change others instead of allowing God to change us. At least, I know that is true in my life."[6]

As we learn how to journey with good questions, we develop raw spirituality. By wrestling with the information or inputs that we receive through questions, we move from information to transformation. Questions are helpful in this movement toward transformation.

In this book we have explored the primary questions around each rhythm:

- Number 1: What is my current picture of God?
- Plug: How are you plugging into God?
- Bread and wine: Who are your companions that you journey with?
- Puzzle: How am I a gift to the world through my unique contribution?

- Shoes: Whose shoes am I called to wear?

- Downward mobility: How can I serve with the resources and privileges that I have?

- Clock: How can I work out my salvation in my job, ministry, work and life?

Although each rhythm has a primary question, we can explore an endless variety of further questions. Many books and resources have question sections, and as I confessed in the beginning of this book, the temptation is to skip these. Once you have established your rhythms and symbols, and populated the different inputs (or curriculums) around it, I encourage you to develop some questions underneath each rhythm.

As we develop questions, it might be helpful to remember the difference between open and closed questions. Open questions help us to discover the journey with another person. It protects people from manipulation. An open question helps a person to explore. You know you have asked an open question when you don't know the answer before you ask it. "What energizes you at the moment?" is an open question.

The opposite end of the spectrum is a closed question. "Don't you think all your series watching saps your energy?" might give you a yes or no answer, but it will not help the person to explore the deeper regions of the soul. There is obviously a place for closed questions. Jesus used both open and closed questions.

- Open: "What can I do for you?" (Mark 10:51)

- Closed: "Has anyone by fussing in front of the mirror ever gotten taller by so much as an inch?" (Matthew 6:27)

Christian traditions differ in the kinds of questions they ask. When John Wesley developed Methodism, questions played a vital part. In his small groups that he called "bands," which consisted of five or six same-gender members, they shared life together and trained naked or "without reserve and without disguise."[7]

Wesley's starter questions for each band included

1. What known sins have you committed since our last meeting?

2. What temptations have you met with?

3. How were you delivered?

4. What have you thought, said or done of which you doubt whether it be sin or not?

5. Have you nothing you desire to keep secret?

These questions are hardcore and reveal intent. It is next-level training naked and is quite different from the popular icebreakers found in small group manuals. In the book *Reflecting God* we find a contemporary version of these questions:

1. What spiritual failures have you experienced since our last meeting? What known sins, if any, have you committed?

2. What temptations have you battled with this week? Where do you feel the most vulnerable right now?

3. What temptations have you been delivered from this week? Please share with us how you won the victory.

4. Has the Lord revealed anything to you about your heart and life that makes you want us to join you in taking a second look at what might be sinful attitudes, lifestyle, or motivations?

5. Is there any spiritual problem that you have never been able to talk about to us or even to God?[8]

Without an integrated understanding of grace these questions can easily lead to frustration or pharisaism. However, as we are grounded in the foundation of grace through the life, death and resurrection of Jesus, these questions can lead us into an adventurous life toward holiness. This brings us to the next part of learning Jesus—designing exercises.

Over the years we have experimented with additional questions (see the group exercise at the end of this chapter) to help us with the different rhythms. As you continue developing raw spirituality, I encourage you to develop questions for your specific context and, if you feel at liberty, to share them with us on our website (rawspirituality.org).

EXERCISES

At the end of every chapter I have introduced a specific exercise. Just as Walter gave me different calisthenics, so we are invited into means of grace, or exercises. Again, I need to confess that I usually speed read through the exercise section of most books or forget the suggestions made in sermons. This is detrimental to growth. Exercises help in developing a range of motions or calisthenics (literally "beautiful strength" or "grace of movement"). As I train with the exercises I become the kind of person who habitually lives these rhythms without even thinking. In other words, the exercises help me to become a different kind of person.

Training helps me toward what Dallas Willard outlines: "Routine, easy obedience to Christ *with reference to specific actions* . . . is the natural outcome of the transformation of the essential dimensions of our personality into Christlikeness."[9] Through our training we allow space for God's Spirit to transform us into people who resemble God's attributes.

Through millennia the church developed various exercises that help us learn Jesus. In his brilliant book *Desiring the Kingdom* theologian and philosopher James K. A. Smith describes these exercises as liturgies. He notes that a liturgy "trains us as disciples precisely by putting our bodies through a regimen of repeated practices that get hold of our heart and 'aim' our love toward the kingdom of God."[10]

These liturgies serve as the bedrock of our exercises. With the liturgical calendar we train our bodies in the church seasons of Advent, Epiphany, Lent, Pentecost and Ordinary Time. During each of these seasons we can focus on specific rhythms. During Advent we celebrate Jesus' incarnation, and it might be a good time to explore the rhythms of the shoes. With Epiphany we can explore our #1 rhythm, our pictures of God. Lent usually focuses on the disciplines of almsgiving, prayer and confession, and might be a good time for focusing on downward mobility and the plug rhythm. During Pentecost we celebrate the Spirit's empowering work and the gifts of the Spirit—a fantastic opportunity to work with the puzzle rhythm. In ordinary time we can explore "working it out" and "bread and wine." There are endless possibilities.

The church also possesses rich treasures in its Sunday service's liturgical cadences (the call to worship, greeting, reading of the law, confession, baptisms, reading the creed, prayer, sermons, Eucharist and sending out of witnesses). Although these liturgies have been associated with certain denominations and high church traditions, they embody the church's collective wisdom on liturgical rhythms that feed into healthy spirituality.

In our continual engagement with a raw spirituality we continue to develop different exercises under each rhythm. We remember the SMART principle discussed in chapter three. These days, most books have wonderful exercises, so in many cases we don't have to reinvent the wheel. A wonderful example of this is the Apprentice Series that contains twenty-nine soul-training exercises.

As we create and develop different exercises, we share them with each other for encouragement and for the stimulation of new imaginative exercises. The website (rawspirituality.org) contains wonderful examples of these.

COMMUNITY

It is really hard to exercise without a buddy. Friendships make exercise enjoyable. When I exercise with a friend, we benefit from mutual support and encouragement. On those days when I drag my feet, my friend gives me a boost and inspires me to stay active. Raw spirituality cannot be cultivated singly. We need to do it in gangs. When Paul wrote to the community in Thessalonica he instructed, "So speak encouraging words to one another. Build up hope so you'll all be together in this, no one left out, no one left behind. I know you're already doing this; just keep on doing it" (1 Thessalonians 5:11).

FORMATION FOR THE SAKE OF THE WORLD

A few years ago two of my friends from Oasis, Kutloano and Anathi, sat with a pastor in a restaurant in a Caesarea Philippi kind of place. The pastor heard about the rhythm of life and asked my friends to explain how they were learning Jesus. They explained the rhythms to the pastor, and he scribbled the symbols of the rhythm along with the questions on a piece of napkin.

A few weeks later a man phoned the pastor with an unusually frank request. "Pastor, I want to come and see you because I don't know how the heck to be a Christian. Can I come?"

The pastor agreed to see him.

When the man entered the pastor's study, he told his story. He was recently divorced and lived in a townhouse complex with some of his friends who were also divorced. After the divorce he started drinking, and this led to violent behavior. During one of his binges he had a racial altercation with someone living in the same complex. His life was spiraling out of control.

"How do I live like a Christian?"

The pastor took out his napkin and gave the rhythm of life a test drive. He carefully explained every rhythm with its symbol and question. The man frantically scribbled the information on the back of a cigarette box.

A few months later the same man phoned the pastor again. "Pastor,

I need to talk to you. This stuff is changing my life. Can I come and see you?"

The man told the pastor that he shared his cigarette-catalogued thoughts with his friends around a barbecue fire. All of his friends had some bad experiences with church or Christianity. As they warmed themselves at the fire, he challenged them, "Boys, we all know that we are not living the Jesus life. I think it is high time that we start to live the stuff Jesus said we should do. So which one of these rhythms should we start with?"

The three of them were all involved in the racial incident and one of them responded, "That's easy. We are racists. Jesus doesn't like that."

The other friends agreed. So they asked the question, Whose shoes are we called to climb into?

Without hesitation they decided that they had to make it right with the men they accosted a few weeks earlier. They decided to invite them to the barbecue. Now. So they walked toward their apartment. At that moment the men drove into the condo parking lot. The three friends knocked on the car window and the passengers locked their doors. They thought they were in for another fight. But there was no fighting on the agenda.

With tears in his eyes the man told the pastor how they became friends with their enemies and testified to the genius of the Jesus way of reconciliation. The man marveled at the discovery of shared humanity. "They are people just like us! We are becoming friends." It was a raw scene with pulsating spirituality. As he sat in the pastor's office, he shared how he wanted to continue on this journey. He yearned for more of this life. He wanted to learn Jesus and be clothed with Christ.

My hope and prayer is that this book will irritate communities to creatively embody raw spirituality for the sake of the world. I also look forward to continuing to learn Jesus and to be clothed in Christ.

Glory to the Father and the Son and the Holy Spirit. As it was in the beginning, is now, and forever will be.

Training Naked

For Reflection and Discussion

1. What bad experiences have you had with teachers?

2. How have you learned Jesus?

3. What makes Jesus different from other teachers?

4. Why would you want to learn from Jesus?

5. Which one of the four movements (input, questions, exercises, community) do you find the hardest? Why?

6. How would you describe discipleship?

7. Would you describe yourself as a disciple? Why or why not?

8. Where is Jesus asking you to follow him?

Individual Exercise

This exercise consists of three phases.

Phase 1. In this phase you are going to determine your current rhythms. The examen exercise and questions (see "Examen to Identify Training Needs" in this chapter) might be helpful. Take at least a week to ponder your current rhythms.

Phase 2. In this chapter we explored the contextualization of the rhythm of life. How would you contextualize the rhythm in your life? Which rhythms would you add or subtract? Which symbols would you change? What is particularly relevant to your life phase?

Phase 3. Ask someone to be your encourager/training partner and answer the following question during your time together: Which rhythm is God currently at work in and inviting me into? Also decide on a practice/exercise that will be helpful to respond to God's invitation.

GROUP EXERCISE

As a group go through the suggested order of meeting in the appendix
(we adapted this order from Renovaré's *Spiritual Formation Workbook*).
Take at least one meeting to work through the order as it is. Then
adapt it to suit your unique context.

Afterword

My good friend and brother in Christ Tom Smith first began inspiring me by his character. Tom is an authentic, committed and grace-filled apprentice of Jesus. The more we spent time together, the more I was inspired by the way he lives his life, by the wisdom that comes from living a Christ-infused life, and by the love, joy, peace, patience, and kindness that flows out of his soul. Then he let me read an early version of this book, and I was inspired by his writing. I engaged the book, as he suggests, not merely reading it but also applying it by engaging in the practices that he suggests.

I went back through the book and noted all of the places that I highlighted as well as the places where I wrote something in the margin, like an exclamation point or a star or a comment on the beauty of the writing. In doing so I found his teaching to be more than good ideas: it's a serious call to live this raw spirituality. When I put them all together, they formed a kind of benediction, a prayer-filled charge. I will share my favorites using Tom's own excellent words (which I cannot improve but merely repeat):

May we join Tom in spending more time in the "gymnasium of God's grace" as we learn to reject our culture's "gymnasium of greed."

May we begin "drawing healthy pictures of God" by "paying attention to Jesus," learning that to pray "hallowed be your name" means the same as praying "help us to draw healing pictures of you."

May we learn how to "unplug from the energy of food in order to connect with our energetic God" and have the courage to admit that when any desire "becomes disordered and is placed above God, it is time for some unplugging."

May we learn our "belovedness," and may it "pressurize us into the flow of God's stream of love for all people."

May we learn that if we are "church idolaters deeply addicted to the institution," we will need to let a new Christology lead "to our missiology, which will lead to our ecclesiology."

May we explore living out the liturgical year, learning "to follow Jesus on a different timetable and to become part of a bigger story."

May we *repent* (change our minds, *metanoia*) by "patterning our lives to a different picture on the box and joining a different gang," a "gang of goodness to make the world a better place," as we follow Jesus who "partied a beautiful life."

May we, following Jean Vanier, make the "transition from 'the community for myself' to 'myself for the community,'" asking not "How was the service?" but "How is my service?"

May we have less "Bible study groups" and more "Bible doing groups."

May we admit—most of us who are privileged to buy and have time to read this book—that we are indeed rich and quit dodging our call to give with the cop-out that we are simply middle class, and have the courage to live more moderately so that others can enjoy their daily bread, creating a financial planner that will "rhyme us in the rhythm of God's kingdom economics."

May we choose our careers with a "sense of vocation," and not just look for a job to make money.

Finally, may we book our calendars with the words *otium sanctum*, so we may have more *holy leisure* in our lives.

Tom has given us, by instruction and example, the way to live a raw spirituality. Now it is up to us to live it.

God bless you on your journey together.

James Bryan Smith

Acknowledgments

Ubuntu is an African philosophy that states "I am because of who you are." The book you are now reading is a proof of Ubuntu. It was written within the beautiful connectedness of different people.

James Bryan Smith encouraged me to write this book and, along with the Apprentice Institute, extended a hand of friendship. I am so grateful for his nudge. Without it this book would not be here.

Renovaré has been a helpful companion on the journey, and it is a privilege to share their imprint.

I am thankful that InterVarsity Press gave me an opportunity to share my thoughts in this book and want to acknowledge Cindy Bunch and her team for their amazing skill.

I thank Trevor Hudson, Fourie Rossouw, Jacques Bornman, Adri-Marie van Heerden, Ryno Meyer and Thomas Dreyer for reading the manuscript and giving honest and encouraging feedback. I value your friendship.

Thanks to Eugene and Jan Peterson, who helped me and Lollie to rediscover the beauty of Jesus.

I am also grateful for many of our American friends who became our family when we lived in the United States. Thanks to Bob and Linda Kirkeeide, Harold and Debbie Howell, Don and Ruth Pape, Gordon and Cherise Selley, Tom and April Hook, and Tod and Valda Smith.

To the people of Claypot and Oasis, who are journeying with the raw spirituality described in this book, thanks for your companionship throughout the journey. I especially thank the elders of Claypot who wrestled with the development of the rule of life: Adri-Marie van Heerden, Gerald and Christina Holt, Schalk van Heerden, Emtia Grobbelaar, Suzette van Rooyen, Gerrit and Tina Kruger, Jacques and Anne-Marie Kruger, Stanis Antonites, and Lollie Smith. I also value the friendships of Carel and Jean van Westing, and my Brazilian friends Eduardo and Márcia Pedreira.

I am grateful for the churches and ministries who have partnered with us in the last few years. I especially thank Andries Enslin and the people at Alberton Lewensentrum.

My wife, Lollie, is my biggest supporter and fiercest critic. Thanks for your loving presence in my life. I love you for an eternity plus ten minutes. Living this Jesus adventure with you, Tayla and Liam is a sacred privilege.

Last, to our family, thanks for laying a foundation in our lives that we can build on.

I dedicate this book to my children, Tayla and Liam. May you continue to live within the rhythms of the Jesus life.

To God be the glory.

TRAINING
NAKED

~

Encouraging One Another
to Love and Good Deeds

In order to have a good meeting we suggest that you meet in a Caesarea Philippi kind of place. Once you are settled in, nominate someone to read the warmup.

1. Warmup[1]

As a community we're training to become the kind of people who love God and others with all our heart, soul, mind and strength. Through the grace of relationship we are here to encourage one another to become more like Jesus. Jesus loves us. This love is the reason why he invites us to follow in his footsteps and become more like him.

Read the rhythm of life prayer together.	**2. Rhythm of life prayer** By God's grace we seek healthy pictures of God and make God *number one.* By God's grace we set aside time to *plug in* with God. By God's grace we *build relationships* with others. By God's grace we discover what *piece of the puzzle* we are and serve the world with it. By God's grace we learn how to *live in the shoes* of others. By God's grace we pursue *downward mobility*, learning how to be stewards of everything in our lives. By God's grace we work out our salvation in our *job, ministry, work and career.*
During this examen we share our experiences with the rhythm(s) we chose in our previous meeting. These questions help us to explore each rhythm. The facilitator reads all the questions under the rhythms out loud and allows each group member to respond to the question that spoke to him or her. Group members are encouraged to use *I* statements when responding.	**3. Examen Questions**

Figure 2.1

Number One

What is your current picture of God? In what way have you experienced God since our last meeting? Who did you encounter that challenged your picture of God? What helps or hinders you to believe that you are made in God's image? What or who is number one in your life? Who is influencing your identity of belovedness? Which characteristic of God amazes you or frightens you? What is God teaching you?

Figure 3.1

Plugged In

How are you plugging in to God? What experiences of plugging in has God given you? How tired, stressed or worried are you feeling? What is giving you power, strength and rest? When did you feel connected or close to God? Did you experience any insights with Scripture or other disciplines? What was your main influence or inspiration this past week?

Figure 4.1

Bread and Wine

Who are your companions on the journey? What relationship affected you the most since our last meeting? Has there been conflict in your relationships and how did you respond? Which relationships have given you life and which ones drained you? Was there any opportunity to practice hospitality? Is there someone you need to forgive? Is there someone God wants you to reach out to or to be open to? Where do you see God at work in your family (marriage, siblings, parents)?

Figure 5.1

Puzzle

How have you been able to contribute your piece of the puzzle to beautify the world? What spiritual gifts/talents has the Spirit enabled you to exercise? How can your deepest joy meet with people's deepest pain? What are you currently learning or growing in? Where did you witness someone else's gifts at work, and how did you respond to their gifts? Who are you learning from to develop your puzzle piece? Whose gifts are you currently benefiting from? How can you show appreciation to them?

Figure 6.1

Shoes

What opportunities has God given you to be in other people's shoes? What is happening in your immediate community? How have you encountered injustice or oppression of others? How were you able to work for justice and peace? Is there any space that you can beautify? Who are you imitating? Where did you notice poverty this week? Did God enable you to be a voice for someone? Have you received from people that wear other shoes? What are some world issues or your country's issues that are breaking your heart? How can you respond?

Figure 7.1

Downward Mobility

How have you served with the privileges and resources that you have? What has God made you a steward of? What are you challenged about and called to share? What dominated your attention and time the most this week? In what way can you be creative with sharing what you have? What is God calling you to do more or less of? Where have you experienced God's generosity? What did you sacrifice in this week (time, opportunity, gifts)? Who made a demand on your life?

Figure 8.1

Clock

Where have you seen God at work in your job, ministry and life? In what ways have you been able to manifest the presence of God through your daily work since our last meeting? What is tough at your work? How is God's kingdom made visible through your work? What and who is dominating your time? What are the effects of the way you work and spend your time at the moment? Where did you experience tension in your work? What did you notice during your commute to work? What rhythms or habits helped you to be present at your work?

Allow time for each member to share his or her plans for the coming week. Writing these commitments down will help you remember what others are doing and give you a chance to pray for them.

4. Training for the Next Weeks

In which of the rhythms (not more than two) do you sense an invitation from God? What specific exercises would you like to experiment with as a response? How can we help you to do this?

After each person has had a chance to share, the leader asks if anyone in the group has a particular need or knows of situations that would benefit from prayer. When the prayer is finished, members join hands in a circle and pray The Lord's Prayer aloud and in unison.

5. The Lord's Prayer

Our Father, who art in heaven,
Hallowed be Thy name.
Thy kingdom come,
Thy will be done on earth, as it is in heaven.
Give us this day our daily bread;
And forgive us our trespasses
As we forgive those who trespass against us.
And lead us not into temptation,
But deliver us from evil.
 For Thine is the kingdom, and the power,
and the glory forever and ever.
Amen.

Notes

INTRODUCTION

[1]Emmanuel M. Katongole and Jonathan Wilson-Hartgrove, *Mirror to the Church: Resurrecting Faith After Genocide in Rwanda* (Grand Rapids: Zondervan, 2009), p. 99.

[2]James K. A. Smith, *Desiring the Kingdom: Worship, Worldview, and Cultural Formation* (Grand Rapids: Baker Academic, 2009), p. 226.

[3]Marjorie J. Thompson, *Soul Feast: An Invitation to the Christian Spiritual Life* (Louisville: Westminster John Knox Press, 2005), p. 146.

CHAPTER 1: TRAINING NAKED

[1]Frederick W. Danker and Walter Bauer, *A Greek-English Lexicon of the New Testament and Other Early Christian Literature,* 3rd ed. (Chicago: University of Chicago Press, 2000), p. 208.

[2]Robert T. Coote and John R. W. Stott, eds., *Down to Earth: Studies in Christianity and Culture* (Grand Rapids: Eerdmans, 1980), p. 7.

[3]Dallas Willard, *Hearing God: Developing a Conversational Relationship with God* (Downers Grove, IL: InterVarsity Press, 2012), p. 254.

[4]Dallas Willard, *The Great Omission* (New York: HarperCollins, 2009), p. 62.

[5]"Grace is God acting in our lives to accomplish what we cannot do on our own." Dallas Willard, *Personal Religion, Public Reality? Towards a Knowledge of Faith* (New York: Hodder & Stoughton, 2009), p. 185.

[6]Søren Kierkegaard, *Provocations: Spiritual Writings of Kierkegaard,* ed. Charles E. Moore (Farmington, PA: Plough, 1999), p. 84.

[7]Dallas Willard, *The Divine Conspiracy: Rediscovering Our Hidden Life in God* (New York: HarperCollins, 1998), p. 25.

[8]Alan Kreider, "Worship and Evangelism in pre-Christendom," presented at the Laing Lecture, London Bible College, 1994, p. 19.

[9]"Mothers Asked Nearly 300 Questions a Day, Study Finds," *Telegraph,* March 28, 2013, www.telegraph.co.uk/news/uknews/9959026/Mothers-asked-nearly-300-questions-a-day-study-finds.html.

[10]Gary Thomas, *Sacred Parenting: How Raising Children Shapes Our Souls* (Grand Rapids: Zondervan, 2009), p. 21.

CHAPTER 2: JESUS WITH A SIX-PACK

[1]Thanks to Alan Hirsch, who pointed me to this cultural drawing of Jesus in Michael Frost and Alan Hirsch, *ReJesus: A Wild Messiah for a Missional Church* (Peabody, MA: Hendrickson, 2009).

[2]"'There's Probably No God . . . Now Stop Worrying and Enjoy Your Life': Atheist Group Launches Billboard Campaign," *Mail Online*, January 7, 2009, www.dailymail.co.uk/news/article-1106924/Theres-probably-God--stop-worrying-enjoy-life-Atheist-group-launches-billboard-campaign.html.

[3]Jay, "Banksy Unmasked," *Visionary Artistry Mag*, March 7, 2011, http://vision aryartistrymag.com/2011/03/banksyunmasked.

[4]Steve Biko, *I Write What I Like: A Selection of His Writings*, ed. Aelred Stubbs (Portsmouth, NH: Heinemann, 1987), p. 56.

[5]Dallas Willard wrote a brilliant essay on this titled "Jesus the Logician," Dallas Willard (blog), June 3, 2013, www.dwillard.org/articles/artview.asp?artID=39.

[6]David Jacobus Bosch, *A Spirituality of the Road* (Scottdale, PA: Herald Press, 1979), pp. 86-87.

CHAPTER 3: GOT POWER?

[1]David L. Turner and Darrell L. Bock, *Matthew, Mark*, Cornerstone Biblical Commentary, ed. Philip W. Comfort (Wheaton, IL: Tyndale House, 2006), p. 415.

[2]Kenneth Samuel Wuest, *Wuest's Word Studies from the Greek New Testament for the English Reader* (Grand Rapids: Eerdmans, 1973), p. 39.

[3]Henri J. M. Nouwen, *The Way of the Heart: The Spirituality of the Desert Fathers and Mothers* (San Francisco: HarperOne, 1991), p. 31.

[4]Quoted in Harold Myra, *Leaders: Learning Leadership from Some of Christianity's Best* (Nashville: W Publishing, 1987), p. 44.

[5]I heard this story in a personal conversation with Eugene Peterson.

[6]James R. Edwards, *The Gospel According to Mark* (Grand Rapids: Eerdmans, 2002), pp. 66-67.

[7]Desmond Tutu, quoted in John Allen, *Desmond Tutu: Rabble-Rouser for Peace* (New York: Simon & Schuster, 2006), p. 154.

[8]Edwards, *Gospel According to Mark*, p. 66.

[9]Trevor Hudson, *A Mile in My Shoes: Cultivating Compassion* (Nashville: Upper Room, 2005), pp. 85-100.

[10]I want to thank Trevor Hudson for personally alerting me to Tutu's delightful phrase "God pressure."

[11]Desmond Tutu and Mpho A. Tutu, *Made for Goodness: And Why This Makes All*

the Difference (New York: HarperOne, 2010), p. 170.

CHAPTER 4: IRRITATING ONE ANOTHER

[1]Max Lucado, *Max on Life: Building a Godly Home* (Nashville: Thomas Nelson, 2007), p. 30.

[2]Edward Abbey, quoted in James M. Cahalan, *Edward Abbey: A Life* (Tucson: University of Arizona Press, 2003), p. 38.

[3]Eugene H. Peterson, *Under the Unpredictable Plant: An Exploration in Vocational Holiness* (Grand Rapids: Eerdmans, 1994).

[4]Alan Hirsch, *The Forgotten Ways Handbook: A Practical Guide for Developing Missional Churches* (Grand Rapids: Brazos, 2009), p. 90.

[5]Henri J. M. Nouwen, *Letters to Marc About Jesus: Living a Spiritual Life in a Material World* (New York: HarperOne, 1998), p. 7.

[6]Elton Trueblood, *Alternative to Futility* (New York: Harper, 1948), p. 43.

[7]Ibid., p. 49.

[8]James Bryan Smith, *The Good and Beautiful Community: Following the Spirit, Extending Grace, Demonstrating Love* (Downers Grove, IL: InterVarsity Press, 2010), p. 78.

[9]Tom Smith, "Operation Mend the Pot," Soulgardeners (blog), November 28, 2003, www.soulgardeners.com/blog/operation_mend.

[10]Clinton E. Arnold, "Early Church Catechesis and New Christians' Classes in Contemporary Evangelicalism," *Journal of the Evangelical Theological Society*, 74, no. 1 (2004), www.etsjets.org/files/JETS-PDFs/47/47-1/47-1-pp039-054_JETS.pdf.

[11]Smith, *Good and Beautiful Community*, p. 190.

[12]Wendell Berry, *The Art of the Commonplace: The Agrarian Essays of Wendell Berry* (Berkeley, CA: Counterpoint Press, 2002), p. 106.

[13]David Arthur DeSilva, *Perseverance in Gratitude: A Socio-Rhetorical Commentary on the Epistle "To the Hebrews"* (Grand Rapids: Eerdmans, 2000), p. 335.

[14]We got the *irritate* idea from W. Vine and F. F. Bruce, *Vine's Expository Dictionary of Old and New Testament Words* (Old Tappan, NJ: Revell, 1981), 2:234.

[15]Dietrich Bonhoeffer, *Life Together: The Classic Exploration of Faith in Community* (New York: HarperOne, 1978), p. 27.

[16]Go to www.challies.com/resources/visual-theology-one-another for a helpful visualization of the "one another" passages.

CHAPTER 5: PUZZLING THE CITY

[1]Donald Miller, *A Million Miles in a Thousand Years: How I Learned to Live a Better Story* (Nashville: Thomas Nelson, 2009), p. xiii.

[2]Rumi, quoted in Peter Scazzero, *Emotionally Healthy Spirituality* (Nashville: Thomas Nelson, 2011), p. 89.

[3]Ralph Waldo Emerson, quoted in Stephen R. Covey, *The Seven Habits of Highly Effective People: Restoring the Character Ethic* (New York: Simon & Schuster, 1990), p. 22.

[4]Stephen B. Bevans and Roger Schroeder, *Constants in Context: A Theology of Mission for Today* (Maryknoll, NY: Orbis, 2004), p. 8.

[5]Jean Vanier, *Community and Growth: Our Pilgrimage Together* (Mahwah, NJ: Paulist Press, 1989), p. 55.

[6]Craig Blomberg, *First Corinthians*, The NIV Application Commentary (Grand Rapids: Zondervan, 1995), p. 248.

[7]Frederick Buechner, *Wishful Thinking: A Seeker's ABC*, rev. ed. (New York: HarperOne, 1993).

[8]Peter Block, *Community: The Structure of Belonging* (San Francisco: Berrett-Koehler, 2009), p. 208.

[9]Ibid., p. 213.

[10]Trevor Hudson and Stephen D. Bryant, *Listening to the Groans: A Spirituality for Ministry and Mission* (Nashville: Upper Room, 2007). This is a beautiful exploration of the process of becoming a loving presence.

[11]*The Epistle of Mathetes to Diognetus* 5, *Early Christian Writings*, accessed April 30, 2012 www.earlychristianwritings.com/text/diognetus-roberts.html.

CHAPTER 6: JESUS MOCCASINS

[1]Alan Hirsch, *The Forgotten Ways: Reactivating the Missional Church* (Grand Rapids: Brazos, 2006), p. 135.

[2]Søren Kierkegaard, *Provocations: Spiritual Writings of Kierkegaard*, ed. Charles E. Moore (Farmington, PA: Plough, 1999), p. 83.

[3]Stephan Joubert, *Hijacked by Jesus* (Vereeniging, South Africa: Christian Art, 2011), p. 18.

[4]Leon Morris, *The Gospel According to John* (Grand Rapids: Eerdmans, 1995), p. 229.

[5]Kenneth E. Bailey, *Poet and Peasant Through Peasant Eyes: A Literary-Cultural ~roach to the Parables in Luke* (Grand Rapids: Eerdmans, 1983), p. 48.

is more than just an internal flaw of individuals. Racism flows into the

ᵔds of the world. Steve Biko, a young black activist who was killed for his attempt to change the South African neighborhood, defined racism as "discrimination by a group against another for the purposes of subjugation or maintaining subjugation" (Steve Biko, *I Write What I Like: A Selection of His Writings*, ed. Aelred Stubbs [Portsmouth, NH: Heinemann, 1987], p. 25).

[7]C. Peter Wagner, *Your Church Can Grow* (Ventura, CA: Regal Books, 1984), p. 127.

[8]John W. De Gruchy, *The Church Struggle in South Africa* (Minneapolis: Fortress Press, 2005), p. 8.

[9]Andreas J. Köstenberger, L. Scott Kellum and Charles L. Quarles, *The Cradle, the Cross, and the Crown: An Introduction to the New Testament* (Nashville: B&H Publishing, 2009), p. 96.

[10]Henry David Thoreau, *Walden: And, on the Duty of Civil Disobedience* (London: Bibliolis, 2010), p. 67.

[11]Brian Fikkert and Steve Corbett, *When Helping Hurts: How to Alleviate Poverty Without Hurting the Poor . . . and Yourself* (Chicago: Moody Press, 2012).

[12]Henri J. M. Nouwen, *Gracias! A Latin American Journal* (New York: Harper & Row, 1983), p. 16.

Chapter 7: Downward Mobility

[1]Oliver James, *Affluenza: How to Be Successful and Stay Sane* (London: Vermilion, 2007), p. vii.

[2]Josh Halliday, "Saudi Prince Launches Libel Action Against Forbes Magazine over Rich List," *Guardian*, June 6, 2013, www.guardian.co.uk/media/2013/jun/06/saudi-prince-libel-action-forbes-rich-list.

[3]Eugene H. Peterson, *Tell It Slant: A Conversation on the Language of Jesus in His Stories and Prayers* (Grand Rapids: Eerdmans, 2012), p. 62.

[4]"His speech is not sad, rather it is pitiful. This wealthy, self-confident man has arrived, he has made it. . . . He needs an audience for his arrival speech. Who is available? Family? Friends? Servants and their families? Village elders? Fellow landowners? . . . The gregarious Middle Easterner always has a community around him. But this man? He can only address himself." Kenneth E. Bailey, *Poet and Peasant Through Peasant Eyes: A Literary-Cultural Approach to the Parables in Luke* (Grand Rapids: Eerdmans, 1983), p. 66.

[5]Cyprian, *Treatises*, Fathers of the Church 36 (Washington, DC: Catholic University of America Press, 2010), p. 138.

[6]Fyodor Dostoyevsky, *The Brothers Karamazov*, trans. Constance Garnett (New York: Spark Educational, 2004), p. 61.

[7]Henri J. M. Nouwen, *Here and Now: Living in the Spirit,* 10th ed. (New York: Crossroad, 2006), p. 120.

[8]Robert A. Stein and Robert H. Stein, *Luke,* The New American Commentary (Nashville: B&H Publishing, 1992), p. 352.

[9]Clement of Alexandria, *Christ the Educator,* Fathers of the Church 23 (Washington, DC: Catholic University of America Press, 2010), p. 126.

[10]Ibid.

[11]Ibid.

[12]Laurie Goodstein, "Senator Questioning Ministries on Spending," *New York Times,* November 7, 2007, www.nytimes.com/2007/11/07/us/07ministers.html?ref=us&_r=o.

[13]Martin Luther, *Martin Luther's Large Catechism and Small Catechism* (Sioux Falls, SD: NuVision, 2007), p. 110.

[14]"Shebeen," *OxfordDictionaries.com,* accessed May 20, 2013, http://oxforddictionaries.com/us/definition/american_english/shebeen

[15]Ray Mayhew, "Embezzlement: The Corporate Sin of Contemporary Christianity?" *TheRelationalTithe.com,* accessed May 23, 2013, www.relationaltithe.com/pdffiles/EmbezzlementPaper.pdf. See also Justo L. González, *Faith and Wealth: A History of Early Christian Ideas on the Origin, Significance, and Use of Money* (Eugene, OR: Wipf & Stock, 2002).

[16]Emmanuel Katongole, "Christianity, Tribalism, and the Rwandan Genocide: A Catholic Reassessment of Christian 'Social Responsibility,'" *Logos* 8, no. 3 (2005): 83.

[17]Emmanuel M. Katongole and Jonathan Wilson-Hartgrove, *Mirror to the Church: Resurrecting Faith After Genocide in Rwanda* (Grand Rapids: Zondervan, 2009), p. 140.

[18]William T. Cavanaugh, *Being Consumed: Economics and Christian Desire* (Grand Rapids: Eerdmans, 2008), p. 9.

[19]I am writing this chapter in a middle-class restaurant. Strike that—a restaurant reserved for the rich. I just ate a $10 steak and drank coffee worth $4.

[20]William H. Willimon, *Sinning Like a Christian: A New Look at the Seven Deadly Sins* (Nashville: Abingdon Press, 2013), p. 107.

[21]Richard J. Foster, *Celebration of Discipline,* quoted in Albert Y. Hsu, *The Suburban Christian: Finding Spiritual Vitality in the Land of Plenty* (Downers Grove, IL: InterVarsity Press, 2006), p. 94.

[22]Clement of Alexandria, *The One Who Knows God* (Amberson, PA: Scroll, 1990), p. 47.

²³Ibid.

²⁴Ibid.

²⁵Loren Wilkinson, Peter De Vos, and Calvin B. DeWitt, *Earthkeeping in the Nineties: Stewardship of Creation* (Grand Rapids: Eerdmans, 1991), p. 216.

²⁶Corrie ten Boom, "Corrie ten Boom Quotes," *GoodReads*, accessed May 23, 2013, www.goodreads.com/author/quotes/102203.Corrie_ten_Boom.

²⁷This is a paraphrase of Clement of Alexandria, cited in Charles Avila, *Ownership: Early Christian Teaching* (Maryknoll, NY: Orbis, 1983), p. 43. The full quote is "Goods are called goods because they do good, and they have been provided by God for the good of humanity."

CHAPTER 8: WORKING IT OUT

¹C. S. Lewis, *Mere Christianity* (New York: HarperCollins, 2009), p. 177.

²Eugene Peterson, "The Pastor: How Artists Shape Pastoral Identity," in *For the Beauty of the Church: Casting a Vision for the Arts,* ed. W. David O. Taylor (Grand Rapids: Baker, 2010), p. 84.

³Martin Luther, quoted in R. Paul Stevens, *The Other Six Days: Vocation, Work, and Ministry in Biblical Perspective* (Grand Rapids: Eerdmans, 2000), p. 77.

⁴James Waldroop, interview by Alan M. Webber, "Is Your Job Your Calling," *Fast Company*, accessed June 11, 2013, www.fastcompany.com/33545/your-job-your -calling-extended-interview.

⁵Martin Luther, quoted in Mark Buchanan, *The Rest of God: Restoring Your Soul by Restoring Sabbath* (Nashville: Thomas Nelson, 2006), p. 23.

⁶Dallas Willard, cited in Bill Heatley, *The Gift of Work: Spiritual Disciplines for the Workplace* (Colorado Springs: NavPress, 2008), p. 148.

⁷Ibid.

⁸"The participle ἐνεργῶν with the definite article ὁ makes the expression almost equivalent to another name for God ('the One who works mightily'). P. T. O'Brien, *The Epistle to the Philippians: A Commentary on the Greek Text,* New International Greek Testament Commentary (Grand Rapids: Eerdmans, 1991), p. 286.

⁹Timothy Keller, *Every Good Endeavor: Connecting Your Work to God's Work* (New York: Dutton Adult, 2012), p. 22.

¹⁰Eberhard Arnold, "Self-Portraits and Portrayals," *The Early Christians: In Their Own Words,* ed. Eberhard Arnold, rev. ed. (Farmington, PA: Plough, 1998), p. 90.

¹¹You can read more about this in Joseph H. Hellerman, *When the Church Was a*

Family: Recapturing Jesus' Vision for Authentic Christian Community (Nashville: B&H Publishing, 2009), p. 99.

[12]John Ortberg, quoted in Siang-Yang Tan, *Rest: Experiencing God's Peace in a Restless World* (Vancouver, BC: Regent College Publishing, 2003), pp. 25-26.

[13]Eugene H. Peterson, *Working the Angles: The Shape of Pastoral Integrity* (Grand Rapids: Eerdmans, 1987), p. 70.

[14]Ibid., p. 71.

[15]Jürgen Moltmann, "Sabbath: Finishing and Beginning," *Living Pulpit* 4 (1998): 5.

[16]Richard J. Foster, *Celebration of Discipline: The Path to Spiritual Growth*, 3rd ed. (San Francisco: HarperSanFrancisco, 1998), p. 27.

[17]Thanks to James Bryan Smith, who taught me these important truths. See his *The Good and Beautiful God* (Downers Grove, IL: InterVarsity Press, 2009).

CHAPTER 9: LEARNING JESUS

[1]For a great book on this metaphor, check out Mark Scandrette, *Practicing the Way of Jesus: Life Together in the Kingdom of Love* (Downers Grove, IL: InterVarsity Press, 2011).

[2]James K. A. Smith, *The Devil Reads Derrida: And Other Essays on the University, the Church, Politics, and the Arts* (Grand Rapids: Eerdmans, 2009), p. 29.

[3]Larry Warner, *Journey with Jesus: Discovering the Spiritual Exercises of Saint Ignatius* (Downers Grove, IL: InterVarsity Press, 2010), p. 30.

[4]William Harmless, *Desert Christians: An Introduction to the Literature of Early Monasticism*, Kindle ed. (Oxford: Oxford University Press, 2004), p. 172.

[5]Richard Rohr, foreword to John Dear, *The Questions of Jesus: Challenging Ourselves to Discover Life's Great Answers* (New York: Image, 2004), pp. xxi-xxiii.

[6]Ibid.

[7]Gary W. Moon and David G. Benner, *Spiritual Direction and the Care of Souls: A Guide to Christian Approaches and Practices* (Downers Grove, IL: InterVarsity Press, 2004), p. 121.

[8]Gary Cockerill, Wesley Tracy, Donald Demaray, and Steve Harper, *Reflecting God* (Kansas City, MO: Beacon Hill, 2000), p. 133, quoted in ibid.

[9]Dallas Willard, "Spiritual Formation and the Warfare Between the Flesh and the Human Spirit," *Journal of Spiritual Formation and Soul Care* 1, no. 1 (2008): www.dwillard.org/articles/artview.asp?artID=132.

[10]James K. A. Smith, *Desiring the Kingdom: Worship, Worldview, and Cultural Formation* (Grand Rapids: Baker Academic, 2009), p. 33.

TRAINING NAKED EXERCISE

[1]This document was adapted from the Renovaré Order of Meeting, found in James Bryan Smith and Lynda L. Graybeal, *A Spiritual Formation Workbook: Small Group Resources for Nurturing Christian Growth* (San Francisco: Harper-SanFrancisco, 1993), p. 99.

APPRENTICE INSTITUTE™

for Christian Spiritual Formation

Under the leadership of James Bryan Smith, The Apprentice Institute (est. 2009), located at Friends University in Wichita, Kansas, provides educational experiences in the area of Christian spirituality, develops resources for individual and church renewal, and engages in research to advance the field of Christian formation.

VISION
The vision of the Apprentice Institute is the renewal of the world and the Church through the formation of new people and new communities who have begun living a radical Christian life in conformity to the teachings of Jesus, as his apprentices, in the midst of the world, whether in secular or ministry positions.

MISSION
To **educate** the current and next generation of leaders.
To **resource** individuals, churches, pastors and ministries in the work of Christian spiritual formation.
To **research** and **advance** the field of Christian spiritual formation.

PROGRAMS AND EVENTS
- An undergraduate degree (B.A.) in Christian spiritual formation
- Adult learning and training experiences in Christian spiritual formation
- Online courses in Christian spiritual formation
- Annual national conference on Christian formation
- Regional "Good and Beautiful God" conferences (find places and dates on our website)

Begin—or extend—your journey of living as an apprentice of Jesus today.

For more information go to www.apprenticeinstitute.org or email us at info@apprenticeinstitute.org.

FRIENDS
UNIVERSITY

What is Renovaré?

Renovaré USA is a nonprofit Christian organization that models, resources, and advocates fullness of life with God experienced, by grace, through the spiritual practices of Jesus and of the historical Church. We imagine a world in which people's lives flourish as they increasingly become like Jesus.

Through personal relationships, conferences and retreats, written and web-based resources, church consultations, and other means, Renovaré USA pursues these core ideas:

- *Life with God* - The aim of God in history is the creation of an all-inclusive community of loving persons with God himself at the center of this community as its prime Sustainer and most glorious Inhabitant.

- *The Availability of God's Kingdom* - Salvation is life in the kingdom of God through Jesus Christ. We can experience genuine, substantive life in this kingdom, beginning now and continuing through all eternity.

- *The Necessity of Grace* - We are utterly dependent upon Jesus Christ, our ever-living Savior, Teacher, Lord, and Friend for genuine spiritual transformation.

- *The Means of Grace* - Amongst the variety of ways God has given for us to be open to his transforming grace, we recognize the crucial importance of intentional spiritual practices and disciplines (such as prayer, service, or fasting).

- *A Balanced Vision of Life in Christ* - We seek to embrace the abundant life of Jesus in all its fullness: contemplative, holiness, charismatic, social justice, evangelical, and incarnational.

- *A Practical Strategy for Spiritual Formation* - Spiritual friendship is an essential part of our growth in Christlikeness. We encourage the creation of Spiritual Formation Groups as a solid foundation for mutual support and nurture.

- *The Centrality of Scripture* - We immerse ourselves in the Bible: it is the great revelation of God's purposes in history, a sure guide for growth into Christlikeness, and an ever rich resource for our spiritual formation.

- *The Value of the Christian Tradition* - We are engaged in the historical "Great Conversation" on spiritual formation developed from Scripture by the Church's classical spiritual writings.

Christian in commitment, ecumenical in breadth, and international in scope, Renovaré USA helps us in becoming like Jesus. The Renovaré Covenant succinctly communicates our hope for all those who look to him for life:

> In utter dependence upon Jesus Christ as my ever-living
> Savior, Teacher, Lord, and Friend,
> I will seek continual renewal through:
> • spiritual exercises • spiritual gifts • acts of service

RENOVARÉ

Renovaré USA
8 Inverness Drive East, Suite 102 • Englewood, CO, 80112 USA • 303-792-0152
www.renovare.us